GARCÍA LORCA

FOR BEGINNERS®

BY LUIS MARTÍNEZ CUITIÑO

D1440746

ILLUSTRATED BY DELIA CANCELA

Writers and Readers®

Writers and Readers Publishing, Inc.
P.O. Box 461, Village Station
New York, NY 10014
sales@forbeginners.com

Writers and Readers Ltd.
PO Box 29522
London N1 8FB England
begin@writersandreaders.com

Spanish Edition:
García Lorca para principiantes,
published by ERA NASCIENTE SLR
Arce 287 -Buenos Aires (1426) - Argentina

Text and Illustration Copyright ©1999 Era Naciente SLR
Concept and Design Copyright ©2000 Writers and Readers Publishing, Inc.
Translated by Lisa Dillman
Book and Cover Design: Piero
Cover Art: Delia Cancela

A Writers and Readers Documentary Comic Book®
Copyright © 2000
ISBN # 0-86316-290-8
1 2 3 4 5 6 7 8 9 0
Printed in Finland by WS Bookwell

Publishing FOR BEGINNERS® books continuously since 1975

1975: Cuba • 1976: Marx • 1977: Lenin • 1978: Nuclear Power • 1979: Einstein • Freud • 1980: Mao
• Trotsky • 1981: Capitalism • 1982: Darwin • Economists • French Revolution • Marx's Kapital • Food
• Ecology • 1983: DNA • Ireland • 1984: London • Peace • Medicine • Orwell • Reagan • Nicaragua •
Black History • 1985: Marx's Diary • 1986: Zen • Psychiatry • Reich • Socialism • Computers • Brecht
• Elvis • 1988: Architecture • Sex • JFK • Virginia Woolf • 1990: Nietzsche • Plato • Malcolm X •
Judaism • 1991: WW II • Erotica • African History • 1992: Philosophy • Rainforests • Miles Davis •
Islam • Pan Africanism • 1993: Psychiatry • Black Women • Arabs & Israel • Freud • 1994: Babies •
Foucault • Heidegger • Hemingway • Classical Music • 1995: Jazz • Jewish Holocaust • Health Care •
Domestic Violence • Sartre • United Nations • Black Holocaust • Black Panthers • Martial Arts • History
of Clowns • 1996: Opera • Biology • Saussure • UNICEF • Kierkegaard • Addiction & Recovery • I Ching
• Buddha • Derrida • Chomsky • McLuhan • Jung • 1997: Lacan • Shakespeare • Structuralism • Che •
1998: Fanon • Adler • Gandhi • U.S. Constitution • 1999: The Body • Krishnamurti • English Language •
Postmodernism • Scotland • Wales • Castaneda • Gestalt • 2000: Art • Bukowski

Contents

✳ A POET, BOTH AVANT-GARDE AND TRADITIONAL

If it is true that I am a poet by the grace of god—or the devil,—i am also a poet by virtue of technique and effort, and knowing precisely what a poem is.

It has been said of **Federico García Lorca**:

The master of images of beauty, he opens the doors of communication to all bodily senses and superimposes their feelings and conceals their nature.

His avant-garde poems do not fall into the automatism of the French surrealists. A logical intelligence reigns over them.

He blends myth with realism, though these become something else when their contact with the magical plane renders them mysterious and indecipherable.

He uses metaphors which unite astronomical images with insects and minutiae.

1

✳ PLAYWRIGHT

Theatre is the poetry that rises up from the book and becomes human. And in so becoming, it speaks and shouts, cries and despairs.

A people who do not cherish and promote their theatre are, if not yet dead, in the process of dying; just as theatre which does not capture the vibrancy of society, of history, the drama of its people, has no right to call itself a theatre but is only a casino or a place to kill time.

What must not be allowed to continue is this existence of players who mount the stage holding their author's hand. They are hollow characters, utterly empty, written for the pit, and they do not satisfy the gods.

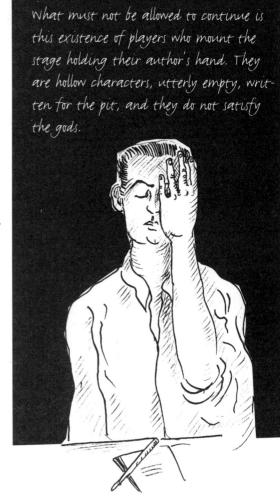

The characters must be so human as to show their flaws; one must note their smell. The boldness of their words, full of love or of hate, must be on their lips.

In theatre the characters must wear the costume of poetry and, at the same time, allow their blood and bones to be seen.

The theatre which has always endured is the theatre of poets, not lyric poets but dramatic poets.

In these times, the poet must lay himself bare before others. That is why I dedicate myself to all things dramatic, which allow a more direct contact with the masses.

A poet must be a teacher of all five senses, and in this order: sight, touch, sound, smell and taste.

As a poet, Lorca was both traditional and avant-garde. His farces, dramas and tragedies are still staged today. But he was also a musician, an artist, singer, orator, actor, director… A complete artist who spoke not to reason, but to the senses of those who read him or attended performances of his plays.

In both his poetry and his theatre, Federico García Lorca lives on, well beyond the parties and tributes given in 1998 to commemorate the hundredth anniversary of his birth.

✳ GRANADA

Granada was Federico García Lorca's homeland. He was born in 1898, the same year that Spain lost its last overseas possessions—most importantly the beautiful island of Cuba—after naval defeat in the Spanish-American War.

4 Trinity Street
Lorca's birthplace

The Moors ruled Granada for eight centuries, until 1492, when they surrendered to the Catholic monarchs. The city still preserves the treasures of the old winter and summer palaces, the Alhambra and the Generalife, respectively. And there is an irrigation system, put in place by adept Moorish engineers to circulate water through the city, that is still in working order. Since this was the site of popular and romantic legends, children learned of its traditions in songs and games. Federico was born in Fuente Vaqueros, in the province rather than the city of Granada. He later moved to Valderrubio.

4

As a young child the poet was unusually attached to nature and spent hours looking at plants and insects.

FE... DE... RI... CO...!

When I was a child, I lived so utterly within nature that I thought poplars spoke, and I could hear their branches calling out my name.

MADAM, THE BOY IS TALKING TO BUGS.

Fuente Vaqueros was a farming town. Federico was the son of a wealthy landowner and, as the first-born, was named after his father. **Federico Lorca Rodríguez**, had remarried after his first wife died, childless. His second wife, Federico's mother, was **Vicenta Lorca Romero**, a spinster who had been the local school-teacher. The couple had three other children: **Francisco, Conchita** and **Isabel**.

5

Federico began his early education with his mother and continued with a kind-hearted teacher, **Antonio Rodríguez Espinosa**, who took a liking to the boy and, according to his brother, Francisco, was the first to notice his great promise. Federico had many relatives who fostered his musical inclination, excellent guitarists and violinists among them. One of his great-uncles became a professional *bandurria* (a Spanish lute-like instrument) player after leaving Fuente Vaqueros, and another exceptionally musically-gifted great-uncle, **Baldomero García Rodriguez**, played several instruments and often sang ballads and songs he had written. His style derived from the *cante jondo* (deep song) of Andalusian gypsy singing. Baldomero was a sort of minstrel who livened up the Lorca family get-togethers.

Federico listened in rapture to his great-uncle, the Flamenco singer, and retained the expression 'black sorrow'.

Another important figure in Federico's cultural heritage was his grandmother on his father's side, **Doña Isabel Rodríguez**. Much given to literature, she read everything from the nineteenth-century poets **José Zorrilla** and **Gustavo Adolf**o **Bécquer** to **Victor Hugo**, for whom she professed boundless admiration. She was very liberal and not overly fond of the Church. Her daughter, Federico's Aunt **Isabel García**, played guitar and was a fine singer. Once, while Federico's mother was in hospital, Aunt Isabel came to look after the children, and she sang to keep them entertained. Federico was soon a huge fan and imitated her with passion.

I asked the moon
what it was you thought about
when, at night, so sad, from
your balcony you looked out.

I climbed up on the wall
the wind thus spoke to me:
why do you give such sighs
if there be no remedy?

The first real display of Federico's dramatic calling was seen in his passion for the liturgy. He used to imitate a priest at mass, bedecked in old clothes made to look like a surplice.

His family encouraged this dramatic inclination by giving him a puppet theatre. Federico then made his friends and family watch the many performances he staged.

Playing with the toy theatre, Lorca proved he was destined for the stage. In addition to the plays he invented and performed with his friends about Jesus, he began to aspire to greater things as he grew older. In 1909 his family moved to Granada. There, Federico attended the Sacred Heart of Jesus School. He also went to the General and Technical Institute (where he failed repeatedly) in the mornings. He failed part of his school-leaving exam as well.

I JUST CAN'T SEE HOW THIS COULD HAVE HAPPENED! I STUDIED REALLY, REALLY HARD!

SON, HOW COULD YOU?

Still, in 1915 he somehow succeeded in finishing secondary school and then started a degree and studied philosophy, literature and law at the university. Thanks to the understanding of his friend **Mora Guarnido** and to the leniency of several of his professors, Lorca managed to scrape through and graduate with a degree in law in 1923. Both in secondary school and at university he met teachers who, while perhaps not leading him to a dedicated life of study, would later be the inspiration for characters in his plays; this was particularly true of Don Martín in *Doña Rosita the Spinster*. The political economy professor in the play was based on Don Ramón Guixé y Mexía.

THE PEOPLE, THE PEOPLE, THE PEOPLE.

GET OFF, YOU MORON!

Law was not the only subject that held no interest for the poet. His courses in the Faculty of Philosophy and Letters left him cold as well.

He did, however, greatly admire Professor **Martín Domínguez Berrueta**, who taught the Theory of Literature and Art. At the end of each term Berrueta would organise a trip to old Spanish cities (Avila, Burgos, Zamora, Salamanca, Baeza, Soria) with his students.

Professor Berrueta is believed to have been a determining force in Federico's vocation as a writer.

Around 1916 Lorca began his first nocturnal scribblings: poems, brief acts and short narratives. He spent his days taking music lessons and going to university lectures.

There is no doubt that the 'literary excursions' organised by Berrueta motivated the first prose pieces the poet later collected in a book.

Impressions and Landscapes came out in 1918, dedicated to Lorca's music teacher, the late **Antonio Segura Mesa**, and financed by his father.

Lorca and Berrueta began to drift apart, and the former's passion for music led him to start meeting with the composer **Manuel de Falla**, who lived with his sister in a garden villa in Granada.

Falla advised Lorca to continue his music studies in Paris, but his father absolutely refused to allow it. Federico decided, therefore, to pursue theatre and poetry. In 1919 he went to Madrid, where he stayed for a time before returning to Granada. He later returned to Madrid once more, after securing a place in the famous **Residencia de Estudiantes**, to continue studying Literature. At that time, Spain's *crème de la crème*— the film director **Luis Buñuel**, the critic **Enrique Díez-Canedo**, the poet **José Moreno Villa** and many others—lived there. Federico immediately became the centre of attention, attracting one and all with his music and poetry. He spent hours playing the piano and would end up surrounded by students.

The lads from Monleón
went off early to plough
—alas, alas—
went off early to plough.

AND WHERE'S THIS ONE FROM? LET'S SEE IF ANYONE CAN GUESS.

THAT'S FROM THE SALAMANCA AREA.

YES, INDEED. VERY GOOD.

IT'S IN FATHER LEDESMA'S SONG-BOOK.

FANTASTIC! WELL SPOTTED, LAD.

Federico lived in the Residencia for nine years.

Living in the Residencia meant regular
contact with students and intellectuals…
and unforeseen encounters, too.

Lorca would become an unconditional admirer of the young genius, **Salvador Dalí**.
He also fell in love with the painter's masculine beauty, which Dalí was well aware
of possessing although he insisted on dressing up as Queen Nefertiti. Following the
carefree, happy days at the Residencia, Lorca and Dalí's friendship grew and
matured. The poet adored the painter. But Dalí's envy at Lorca's success eventually
brought distance between the two men.

BOOK OF POEMS

Oh, strong woman of ebony and of nard!,
with breath as white as bishop's-weed.
Venus of the Manila shawl who knows
of sweet Malaga wine and of guitar.

In many of the poems that appeared in **Book of Poems**, Federico's first collection (1921), typically Lorquian characters can already be seen emerging. In 'Elegy', for example, we see the frustrated woman who was to become paramount in future plays: the spinster who grows old waiting for a man who never arrives, or who doesn't return.

No one makes you flower, Andalusian martyr
your kisses should have been beneath the vine
full of the silence contained in the night
and of the muddy rhythm of stagnant waters.

But the circles beneath your eyes grow
and your black hair turns to silver;
your breast slips down, spilling aromas
and your lovely spine now curves over.

Doña Rosita the spinster might be the character most easily recognisable here, but there are also allusions, as we will see, to the sterility of the heroine of **Yerma**.

15

FIRST THEATRICAL ENDEAVOURS

The Butterfly's Evil Spell was the play that, in 1920, launched Lorca's theatrical career. The director and playwright, **Gregorio Martínez Sierra** accepted the script and directed the play; his wife **Catalina Bárcena** played the lead. It ran for all of two days and was a resounding fiasco. The storyline was simple: a wounded butterfly falls into a field of cockroaches; one of them, a poet, Curianito, falls in love with her, but when the butterfly regains her flight she leaves him. The butterfly symbolised the ideal, and Curianito the search for the ideal.

POEM OF THE DEEP SONG

In 1922, Federico and Manuel de Falla organised a *cante jondo* competition. The pair had spent Holy Week in Seville, and the festivities there intensified Falla's desire to rescue this soulful form of folk expression from what he saw as its incipient demise.

That contest turned out
to be a way of both
revitalising and docu-
menting the tradition.

This enthusiasm for the song and the gypsies' innate understanding of mythology resonated with the poet, stirring within him a neopopulism that led to two books of poetry: **Poem of the Deep Song** and **Gypsy Ballads**. Both works were imbued with the spirit of a race on the margins of history. The real significance of the first of these books, however, lay in the abundance of geometric lines, upon which Lorca placed poetic images that appealed to the senses, to the collective unconscious: the cross, or the zigzag of a lightning bolt, for example. In these, ancient shapes act as reminders of the primitive drawings found in early civilisations. The orthogonality (that is, the meeting of perpendicular lines) makes the vertical of life meet the horizontal of death. Thus, in 'Death's Lament', the candlestick and the blanket on the ground imply man's difficulty in accepting death:

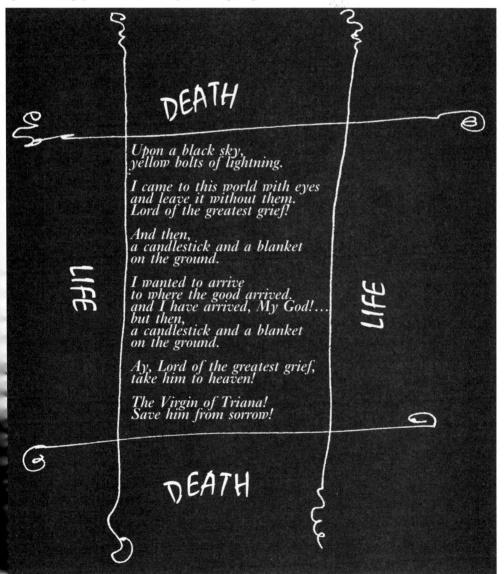

DEATH

LIFE
LIFE

Upon a black sky,
yellow bolts of lightning.

I came to this world with eyes
and leave it without them.
Lord of the greatest grief!

And then,
a candlestick and a blanket
on the ground.

I wanted to arrive
to where the good arrived.
and I have arrived, My God!...
but then,
a candlestick and a blanket
on the ground.

Ay, Lord of the greatest grief,
take him to heaven!

The Virgin of Triana!
Save him from sorrow!

DEATH

The refrain—'a candlestick and a blanket on the ground'—came from a famous Flamenco singer, **Juan Breva**:

YOU'RE SUCH A SCEPTIC. IT'S REALLY BECOMING QUITE UNBEARABLE!

THAT DOESN'T MEAN YOU CAN'T ENJOY IT.

I'M A REALIST; IT'S NOT THE SAME THING. SUCCESS NEVER LASTS. EVERYTHING IN LIFE PASSES.

YES, IT DOES. FOR ME IT DOES, ANYWAY. BECAUSE I THINK THAT JUST WHEN YOU LEAST EXPECT IT, IT ALL ENDS: A CANDLESTICK AND A BLANKET ON THE GROUND.

OH LORD OF GREAT SORROW, RAISE HIM UP TO GLORY.

HOLY VIRGIN OF TRIANA, SAVE HIM FROM ALL PAIN.

In another poem, 'Surprise', a dead man takes the place of the blanket and a dagger replaces the candlestick.

Dead he lay on the street
with a dagger in his chest.
No one knew him.
How the lamp trembled!
Mother.
How the little street lamp
trembled!

WHAT DID THEY DO TO YOU? WHO DID THIS?

At other times, the right-angle is formed by one vertical element, such as a tower, and its horizontal reflection: the same tower reflected, or 'dead', in stagnant water. In the 'Ballad of the Three Rivers' Lorca writes:

Darro, Genil, little towers
dead above the ponds.

Likewise, the orthogonality between the living element and its shadow can be seen in 'Ay!'

The scream leaves on the wind
the shadow of a cypress.

The dead towers and the cypress are charged with a funereal signifi-cance, reinforced by the horizontal reflection of a raised element: something erect that falls to earth.

At the end of the book, Federico drew a cross, and added to it the shadow of its reflection in the water.

The cross is the final point, as well as being the road. This dichotomy between life and death is divided by the poet once more between the cross (full stop) and its reflection (ellipsis). In this case, the parenthetical plane corresponds to linguistic signs; the full stop is death but it is also a punctuation mark. As such, it corresponds to the ellipsis. These both leave a space to be filled as well as suggesting continuity. The water in the ditch is running water, which does not reflect a distinct silhouette, as does the pond water, but rather produces a rippled image that justifies the ellipsis.

The book also offers other lines and universal shapes such as the labyrinth, the wave (serpent, water), the zigzag (lightning), depth (water), etc., which have been around forever and communicate universally. To the contemporary reader, the book is suggestive of something beyond the rational, because it speaks through images.

PUPPET THEATRE
AND *THE BILLY CLUB PUPPETS*

The failure of *The Butterfly's Evil Spell* cost Federico seven years. There was no way for him to get his play *Mariana Pineda* accepted anywhere. He said that after Martínez Sierra rejected it, the play was then turned down by several more houses, given back to him by people full of praise but also fearful— some of how daring it was and others of its difficulty. In the meantime, he worked with his puppet theatre. In 1922, Lorca finished a version of *The Billy Club Puppets: The Tragicomedy of Don Cristobál and Miss Rosita*. It was Lorca's only work in which love succeeds. *The Tragicomedy of Don Cristóbal and Miss Rosita* was not performed until 1937, (after the poet's death) in a performance that used actors instead of puppets. *The Little Puppet Show of Don Cristóbal*, Lorca's farewell to Argentina, was staged with puppets. It had a carefree Punch-and-Judy air that the Tragicomedy, with its intellectual depth, lacked.

The Billy Club Puppets: The Tragicomedy of Don Cristóbal and Miss Rosita is the only one of Lorca's works in which love is rewarded: the heroine ends up marrying her beloved Cocoliche. *The Little Puppet Show of Don Cristóbal* is, on the other hand, a fundamentally sordid story: Doña Rosita is sold off by her mother, who sings Rosita's praises to an elderly Cristóbal.

On Twelfth Night in 1923, Lorca staged *The Girl Who Waters the Basil-Pot and the Inquisitive Prince* at his home in Granada. It was attended by his sister Isabel, her friends, and many of the poor children of the area. The play was based on an Andalusian tale. Lorca himself designed the sets and, with his sister Concha, acted as puppeteer. During intermissions, he brought out the puppet Don Cristóbal to talk to the delighted children. He also performed a Cervantes interlude, *The Two Speakers*, and a medieval mystery called *The Magi*. The orchestra (violin, clarinet, lute and piano, played by Falla) accompanied the plays with selections from Debussy, Albéniz, Ravel and Pedrell. It turned out to be quite an event.

GIRL:

My eyes are blue
and my little heart like
the crest of light.

PRINCE:

Girl who waters the basil,
how many leaves are on the plant?

GIRL:

Tell me quarrelsome king,
how many stars are in the sky?

When the Girl closes the window, the Prince leaves, saddened. He later disguises himself as a fisherman and thus begins a romance with the Girl. She pays for the fish she buys from him with kisses. During the question scene, the Girl asks:

Offended, the Girl closes the window again, and the Prince falls ill. The king's wise men get together to come up with a solution. Aware of this, however, the Girl appears disguised as a wizard wearing a black cape and a pointed hood embroidered with stars. She enters the palace singing:

and she proposes the following as a foolproof remedy:

LORCA IN CADAQUÉS

In 1925, Dalí invited Lorca to spend the Holy Week holidays with him in the Ampurdán. This was Lorca's first visit to Cadaqués where the Dalí family had a seaside house.

Lorca read *Mariana Pineda* to the family.

BRAVO!

BRAVO!

I AM LIBERTY, WOUNDED BY MEN! LOVE, LOVE, LOVE AND ETERNAL SOLITUDE!

YOU ARE THE GREATEST POET OF THE CENTURY!

WELL, THANK YOU! THANK YOU SO MUCH!

Puppet theatre incorporated the obscenities and the swearing of common folks, who used the strong language of the country and amused themselves with vulgar jokes that were rude without being malicious. Lorca's farcical plays were related to traditional farces. **Cervantes** was an expert in the genre; closer to Federico was **Pedro de Alarcón**; and, almost a contemporary, was **Ramón del Valle-Inclán**. Lorca's two most distinguished farces were *The Shoemaker's Prodigious Wife* and *The Love of Don Perlimplín with Belisa in the Garden*.

The Love of Don Perlimplín with Belisa in the Garden, which premièred in April 1933, was subtitled 'An Erotic *Aleluya*'. At the turn of the century, *aleluyas* were long sheets of coloured paper which narrated a story in cartoon form. A caption at the foot of the page would explain each drawing. In Federico's play, the exaggerated comic element represented, at first, what surrounded the original *aleluya*: this was hyperbole which later disappeared, leaving just the musical and exquisite elements to prevail.

THE LOVE OF DON PERLIMPLÍN WITH BELISA IN THE GARDEN

This short piece, with only four scenes, presents the unequal marriage of Perlimplín—a naive man of some fifty-odd years who spends his time studying—and Belisa, a sweet young thing who seems to be nothing but a beautiful body. The maid, Marcolfa, worried about her master's future, convinces him that it is in his interest to marry the young beauty. On their wedding night, Belisa deceives him with five men, who represent the earth's five races.

29

Perlimplín accepts his impotency and his age, and gives Belisa advice about her other lovers. She confesses that she has fallen in love with someone who writes her letters but refuses to show his face. In his most recent letter, the man has confessed that it is her body, trembling and white, rather than her soul which he desires. Marcolfa, under orders from Don Perlimplín, informs Belisa that the young man will come to the garden at ten o'clock that night, wearing a red cloak. At exactly that time, he (Don Perlimplín in disguise) appears.

Belisa calls out to him, but he signals that he will return. Just then, Perlimplín appears as himself, takes out a dagger, and tells her that he is going to kill the young gallant who, once dead, will stay with Belisa forever. He runs off. From between the branches a man appears, draped in a large, luxurious red cape. He is wounded. He hides his face in the folds of his cloak.

BELISA:

MY LOVE! WHO HAS WOUNDED YOU IN THE BREAST? LET ME SEE YOUR FACE, JUST FOR AN INSTANT AY! WHO HAS KILLED YOU?

PERLIMPLÍN:

YOUR HUSBAND HAS JUST KILLED ME WITH THIS EMERALD-STUDDED KNIFE.

BELISA:

PERLIMPLIN!

PERLIMPLÍN:

HE RAN OFF THROUGH THE FIELDS. HE'LL NEVER COME BACK. HE KILLED ME BECAUSE HE KNEW I LOVED YOU LIKE NO ONE ELSE AS HE PLUNGED THE KNIFE INTO MY FLESH, HE SHOUTED: BELISA AT LAST HAS A SOUL! COME CLOSER.

BELISA:

WHAT HAVE YOU DONE?

PERLIMPLÍN:

I AM MY SOUL AND YOU ARE YOUR BODY ALLOW ME IN THIS LAST MOMENT, SINCE YOU HAVE LOVED ME SO, TO DIE EMBRACING IT.

The Shoemaker's Prodigious Wife was first performed on Christmas Eve, 1930, with **Margarita Xirgu** as the heroine.

The young wife, married off to the old shoemaker, does nothing but complain incessantly about the most trifling of matters.

The shoemaker's wife stands at the window and talks to those who pass by, all of whom are suitors. The indignant shoemaker leaves his wife, planning never to return. After playing with a butterfly he wanted to catch, The Boy breaks the news to her and she realises how much she loves her husband. The Boy, the shoemaker's wife's only friend, is the symbol of her frustrated maternal urges. The butterfly symbolises the ideal, which is always far off. And the theme of honour in this first act is a superficial honour. In the second, it is deeper honour. The wife opens a tavern and attends to her customers; the gossiping neighbours pry, make comments and pass judgement as they peer through the window. The hopeful suitors (Youth with Sash, Youth with Hat, Don Blackbird and the Mayor) keep trying to seduce her. They all wish to take advantage of her husband's absence, and she in turn continually keeps them all in line.

A series of couplets that slander the wife are then sung. Meanwhile, the Shoemaker returns disguised as a puppeteer, a trumpet in one hand and a rolled-up scroll behind his back. Here, Lorca uses the 'play-within-a-play' device, first seen in **Pirandello**'s theatre. The puppeteer tells the extravagant story which is painted into squares on his scroll. The story is suspiciously similar to his own.

> RESPECTFUL SPECTATORS, HEAR THE TRUE AND MOVING BALLAD OF THE RUBICUND WIFE AND THE LITTLE MAN OF PATIENCE, THAT IT MAY SERVE AS AN EXAMPLE AND A WARNING TO ALL THOSE OF THIS WORLD. LISTEN CAREFULLY AND GRASP THE MESSAGE:

In Cordoba within a cottage
set about with trees and rose bays,
once upon a time a tanner
lived there with a tanner's wife.
(Expectancy.)

She was a very stubborn woman,
he a man of gentle patience;
though the wife had not turned twenty,
he was then well over fifty.

Good Lord, how they would argue
Look now at that beastly woman,
laughing at the poor weak husband
with her glances and her speaking.

> WHAT A TERRIBLE WOMAN!

Dark hair worthy of an empress
had this little tanner's wife,
and her flesh was like the water
from Lucena's crystal sources.
When she moved her skirts and flounces,
as she walked about in springtime,
her clothes gave off the fragrance
lemon groves and mint exhale.

Oh what lemons, lemons
of the lemon grove!
Oh what a delicious
little tanner's wife!

[The neighbours laugh.]

The performance ends suddenly, and a knife fight breaks out. The neighbours accuse the shoemaker's wife of being the cause. Imprisoned in her house with the puppeteer, whom she protects from the crowd, the wife speaks of people's envy and of how she has to defend herself against those who try to take advantage of her husband's absence. The shoemaker attempts to win her over as well, but is rejected. Overjoyed, he asserts that she has behaved as a true woman.

37

The recognition finally comes at the end. And in spite of the joyful reunion, the girl's bad temper re-emerges and, going to the closed door where the townspeople are chanting offensive couplets she shouts:

RECONQUERING THE STAGE:
MARIANA PINEDA

In early 1926, Federico sent dramatist **Eduardo Marquina** the script of *Mariana Pineda* and asked him to give it to the actress **Margarita Xirgu**. By chance, Xirgu bumped into a friend, Cuban writer **Lydia Cabrera**, in the lobby of the Ritz Hotel, where she was staying; it was thus discovered that Marquina had not carried out Lorca's request. The actress had never even heard of Lorca. Her curiosity was aroused and she asked Lydia to call Marquina and ask for the script. Cabrera had a better idea: she would collect it, as her car was parked just outside the hotel. She didn't give the actress time to stop her. Soon after, she returned, brandishing the play:

Lydia took her to meet Federico the very same day, and the Granadan's warmth immediately charmed Margarita. She promised to read the play and in February 1927, **Rivas Cherif**, director of her theatre company, wrote to tell him that Xirgu would open the play on 24 July, at the Teatro Goya, in Barcelona.

The play was subtitled 'A Popular Ballad in Three Prints'. The 'print' recalled coloured lithographs, old engravings, like those used in the nineteenth century. Lorca was thereby indicating that his theme was stylised, the essence of a historical and literary epoch, but seen through an avant-garde sensibility which would not leave the more delicate aspects untouched. His friend Salvador Dalí designed the sets with tremendously avant-garde sensibilities: the curtains served as mere background for the actors. The colours were on the characters' costumes, so the set itself was nearly monochrome. All the props were drawn and only the windows were real.

AVE MARIA

Oh! What a sad day in Granada,
the stones began to cry;
they could not make Marianita speak
and so she had to die.

Marianita, sitting in her room
thought of one thing only:
'What if Pedrosa saw me weave
the flag of Liberty?'

A Lorca drawing of Marianita sitting in her room.

A girl emerges from the chorus. Dressed in the fashion of 1850, she sings one ballad verse as she crosses the stage:

As a lily they cut the lily
as a rose they cut the flower,
as a lily they cut the lily,
and her soul was even finer.

She enters her house—we later learn that it was Mariana Pineda's house—and the chorus sings the first two lines of the first verse again. At the end of the play another chorus, this time boys, once more sings the two first lines of the ballad's first quartet, after bells are heard tolling.

The play's circular framework has an extraordinary effect: it can begin and end anywhere, like certain childhood 'never-ending stories'. The historical drama appears to be seen from a child's point of view, but this does not diminish the depth with which the author endows it.

'Mariana, so the story goes, was an incredibly passionate woman, crazed, and an exemplary case of magnificent Andalusian love, caught up in political surroundings.'

'What deep emotion trembles in my
eyes at the legend of Marianita...

I've heard that evocative verse ever
since I was a child.'

Marianita went out for a walk
and a soldier came out to meet her
and he said to her:—Ay, my Marianita
there is danger, please turn back.

'This woman had passed through the secret
path of my life. A woman I glimpsed and loved at
nine years of age, when I was travelling from Fuente
Vaqueros to Granada in an old stagecoach, and the
driver played a wild tune on his copper trumpet.'

Inspired by that image which he had held on to since childhood, Federico
wrote the play. Both the critics and the public were unstinting in their praise.
The play was based on the story of Mariana Pineda, a woman who lived in
Granada in the early 1900s, during the tyrannical reign of Ferdinand VII. She
was executed when she was still quite young, leaving behind two small children, for her role in the liberal opposition: refusing to give the names of collab-
orators and embroidering a liberal flag. In 1831, she was garroted.

At the request of the man she loves, Mariana risks embroidering a liberal flag and hides it in a house in the Albaicín gypsy quarter of Granada. Fernando, a boy of eighteen, is in love with Mariana and when he pays her a visit, she asks if there are many people in the streets. He tells her that a military man has escaped from the prison and that troops are pursuing him. Mariana does not hesitate to endanger Fernando's life by asking him to take her lover, Pedro de Sotomayor, a passport and the documents necessary to leave Spain.

47

Lorca juxtaposed young Fernando's disappointment at Mariana's love for Don Pedro with Mariana's own paranoia: she is convinced that the chief of police, Pedrosa, is spying on her through the balcony. In this way, Lorca was trying to get across the idea of the outside prison, which is transferred to the inside of the house, imprisoning Mariana.

In the second Print, the heroine is reunited with Pedro, who takes refuge in her house, and with other conspirators who have come from all over Spain to discuss whether the uprising should take place, given the death of General Torrijos, who had been betrayed. Suddenly there is a loud banging at the door. Mariana, desperate, forces everyone to flee through the back and confronts the fearsome Pedrosa on her own. To hide her nervousness, she pretends to drop her wedding ring and bends down to pick it up. The police chief takes advantage of her position, embracing and kissing her. Indignant, she orders him to leave.

In the last Print, Mariana, having refused to betray her fellow conspirators, is imprisoned in the convent of Santa María Egipciaca. She feels everyone has abandoned her, but waits naively for Pedro to come to her rescue. An air of innocence surrounds her, now heightened by the presence of the convent nuns as it was earlier by the children's songs, games and ballads. Mariana ascends to a higher plane.

Mariana Pineda in the convent of Santa María Egipciaca.

You love liberty more than anything,
but I am that same Liberty. I give my blood,
which is your blood and the blood of all creatures.
The human heart is not for sale!

Now I know of what speak
  the nightingale and the tree.
Man is a captive and cannot be free.
Noble liberty! True liberty,
light your distant stars for me.

Finally, Mariana is led
off to be executed.

LIBERTY

The future will
bring Pineda and
García Lorca
together: both are
victims, sacrificed
to despotism and
political madness.
Their parallel
destinies can be
summed up in
their love of free-
dom.

✳ DRAWINGS

The day after the première of *Mariana Pineda*, Lorca opened an exhibition of his drawings at the Dalmau Galleries in Barcelona, with the support of the owner, and the art critic **Sebastián Gasch**. For the first time, he showed in an art gallery which had always been open to the Spanish, as well as the European, avant-garde. There were twenty-four pictures on display. All of Federico's friends knew that he drew, and he tended to illustrate his letters, books, and inscriptions; sometimes he made his own stage sets. He had been drawing ever since childhood, and always had coloured pencils with him.

Between 1926 and 1928, he illustrated both prose and poems that were published in the Sitges-based Catalan journal *L'Amic de les Arts*, in Malaga's *Litoral*, and in Granada's *Gallo*. *Mariana Pineda* was published with the author's drawings and the *Revista de Occidente* published *Gypsy Ballads*, which he also illustrated. Progressive critics praised his work. Gasch himself said:

> GARCIA LORCA'S DRAWINGS ARE MEANT FOR THOSE WHO ARE PURE AND SIMPLE, THOSE WHO ARE ABLE TO FEEL WITHOUT NEEDING TO UNDERSTAND.

These drawings are both pure poetry
and pure art.

I feel clean, comforted, happy and childlike
when I make them.

I am horrified by what they call direct
painting, which is no more than an
anguished battle with forms in which the
painter always triumphs, leaving the work
dead.

In these abstractions I see more realities created, which join the reality that surrounds
us...

I would call these drawings very human
drawings. Because almost all of them strike
a little arrow in the heart...

...little arrow in the heart...

FEDERICO AND ANA MARÍA DALÍ

Songs (1921-1924) was finally published in May 1927, at the printing house Sur run by the Malaga magazine, *Litoral*. Federico was in Figueras at the time, staying with the Dalí family. His friends from *Litoral* sent a copy there. In the book there was a song dedicated to Ana María Dalí. When the book arrived she was in Cadaqués, and Federico decided to take it to her in person.

One afternoon, Ana María received a message saying that García Lorca would arrive at lunchtime. But when the taxi arrived, it contained only a teddy bear.

Ana María, in tears, took the little bear and entered the house to tell the maid that Federico would not be coming to lunch after all. Suddenly, as if by magic, he appeared, pretending to be very angry.

But Federico suddenly began to laugh heartily.

They spent a splendid day together…

After having lunch in the open air, the pair went for a siesta on the beach and, at nightfall, returned to Figueras. Earlier, they had leafed through *Songs* together and Federico had added to the inscription that his friends at Litoral had written. He wrote:

All at the precious feet of Ana María.

It is very difficult to classify the feelings that Federico and Ana María had for each other. Perhaps it was consummated love. Or did one of the two pull away before it was too late? We will never know. But at the time, Ana María would speak to both her brother and Federico about the most ardent subjects, and she was educated enough to speak to them both as equals. Federico and Ana María's friendship was a love of some kind, but of just which kind remains unclear.

Lorca was a member of what critics call the **'Generation of 27'**, named for the tribute paid by young and notable poets in 1927 to an earlier poet, **Luis de Góngora**, in Seville, three centuries after his death. Along with Lorca, **Jorge Guillén**, **Pedro Salinas**, **Dámaso Alonso**, **Gerardo Diego**, **Vicente Aleixandre**, **Luis Cernuda**, **Rafael Alberti**, **Manuel Altolaguirre** and **José Bergamín** also belonged to the group. The 'Generation' took a renewed interest in folk traditions, which they collected both directly from the people and through rigorous research. The result was a learned popularism, which tended to be quite refined, like Lorca's work. These poets revitalised images and metaphors, which allowed them to glimpse new meaning in things, whether through the intellect or through emotion.

SO, YOU LIKE MY BALLADS, PACO?

The ideas upheld by the Generation of 27 were exemplified in Lorca's most popular and widespread work, the **Gypsy Ballads**, published in 1928: although readers did not completely understand what the poet was talking about, the metaphors and images were so evocative that they appealed to the senses. It was not about grasping the logic of the ballad but about feeling attracted to, even subjugated by, the musical and artistic language the poet used.

Lorca did not like to publish his books immediately after writing them. *Poem of the Deep Song* came out in 1931, almost ten years after it was begun. *Gypsy Ballads*, too, was published in 1928, five years after Lorca began the collection. Some of the ballads were already known, as Federico regularly recited in public. Spectators recalled that hearing him recite was an experience never to be forgotten.

Seville

Federico recited 'The Unfaithful Wife' during the Góngora commemoration with other members of the Generation of 27:

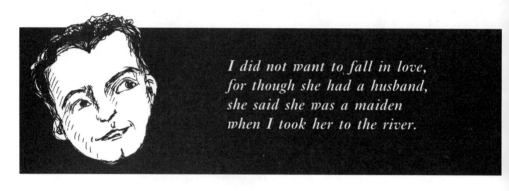

I did not want to fall in love,
for though she had a husband,
she said she was a maiden
when I took her to the river.

A climactic evening. The audience went wild, waving handkerchiefs as at the best bullfights. Federico, moved, thanked them. So over-excited were they that people threw jackets, collars and ties in a state of frenzy.

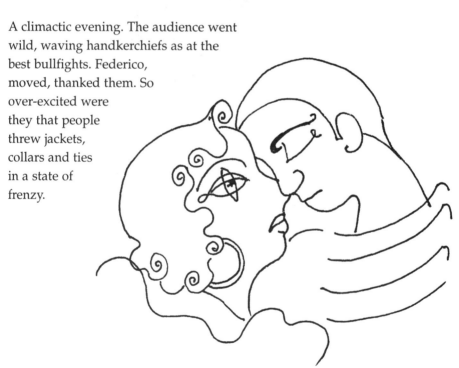

The first editions of *Gypsy Ballads* sold out quickly, and in later years the collection remained equally popular.

...AND WITH THE SAME METRE AND RHYME SCHEME, A DIFFERENT BALLAD CAN BE CREATED. A BALLAD THAT BLENDS THE COSMIC WITH THE MINUSCULE, AND THAT BLENDS MYTH WITH THOSE ELEMENTS WE COULD CALL REALIST. OF COURSE THEY'RE NOT, SINCE BY COMING INTO CONTACT WITH THE MAGICAL PLANE THEY BECOME EVEN MORE MYSTERIOUS AND INDECIPHERABLE.

HAVE YOU DONE RESEARCH INTO GREEK MYTHOLOGY?

YES, THAT'S WHAT ALLOWED ME TO FORGE AND INVENT NEW MYTHS, AND TO BLEND THEM WITH THE ONES I ALREADY KNEW. MYTHS CONNECT MAN TO THE COSMOS. I WANTED TO RECREATE ANDALUSIAN PRIMITIVISM.

Lorca wanted to grasp the complexity of the Andalusian people, who had been invaded by so many diverse cultures: Tartessian, Phoenician, Greek, Carthaginian, Roman and Islamic. The Moors, of course, were there for many centuries as well as the gypsies who arrived in the fifteenth century and settled in the Sierra Nevada. They brought from the East ancient elements that were united with others to create an inner Andalusia. In *cante jondo*, Lorca gave form to the metaphysical sorrow of his land.

Sorrow is the only character the poet spoke of in the *Ballads*. This sorrow is identified with Andalusian anguish in the face of life's great questions.

This sentiment is personified by Soledad Montoya, in the 'Ballad of the Black Sorrow'.

Soledad, whom do you ask for,
alone, at this hour?

SOLEDAD:
Whoever I ask for,
what business of yours?
I search for what I search for,
myself and my joy.

POET:
Soledad of my sorrows,
when a horse runs away,
it finds the sea at last
and is swallowed by waves.

SOLEDAD:
Don't tell me of the sea,
for the black sorrow rises
beneath the murmur of leaves
in the country of olives.

POET:
Soledad, how sad you are!
What pitiful grief!
You weep drops of lemon,
long-stored, sour in the
mouth…

In order to define sorrow, Lorca added other concepts:

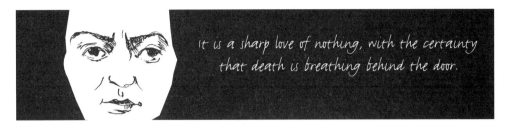

It is a sharp love of nothing, with the certainty that death is breathing behind the door.

Death comes suddenly to interrupt life and is often bloody or related to the cosmos, as in the 'Ballad of the moon, moon'. At other times it is brought on by superstition, as in the 'Ballad of the Doomed Man', which was based on a motif from an old Spanish ballad (sentenced to death by Ferdinand IV for slander, the youngest of the Carvajales family calls the king before God, thirty days from his death). Other ballads, such as the 'Ballad of Santa Olalla', are also based on popular tradition.

Most of the ballads refer to the gypsy world of Andalusia. In the 'Ballad of the Spanish Civil Guard', two civilisations are at odds, the primitive and the contemporary. In others, such as 'Reyerta' and the 'Death of Antoñito el Camborio', violence is prevalent. In the latter, the character holds a conversation with the poet himself:

POET:

Antonio Torres Heredia,
Camborio of hard locks,
dark in the green moon
the manly carnation's voice:
Who took away your life,
beside the Guadalquivir?

ANTONIO:

My four Heredias cousins,
Benamejí's sons.
They did not envy in others
what they envied in me.
[...]

POET:

Ay, Antoñito el Camborio,
worthy of an Empress!
Think about the Virgin
because you are going to die.

ANTONIO:

Ay, Federico García,
call the Civil Guard!
Like a stalk of maize
my waist is snapped.

Desire and sensuality are present in some of the ballads, such as 'The Unfaithful Wife'; in others, for example, 'Sleepwalking Ballad', there are dream-like elements:

With waist of shadow
she dreams at her rail,
green flesh, hair green,
and her eyes, cold silver.
Beneath the gypsy moon,
things are looking at her,
and she can't look at them.
[…]

The fig tree chafes its wind
with its sandpapered branches,
and the mountain, untamed cat,
bristles sour maguey spears.

But who will come? From where?
Still she leans on her rail,
green flesh, hair green
dreaming of the bitter sea.

LORCA:

> THE GYPSY FLOATING
> IN THE WELL IS DEAD.

That's why her eyes are cold and there are things that she cannot look at. The reflection comes from the rail that she threw herself from; now she 'dreams'. Green impregnates the entire poem.

JOURNALIST:

> WHAT DOES GREEN FLESH SUGGEST? MAYBE IT'S THE BODY
> BEGINNING TO DECOMPOSE?

LORCA:

> IT MIGHT ALSO BE THE COLOUR OF THE RAIL
> OR SOMETHING ELSE ENTIRELY.

In this, Lorca's most famous book, he transcends the gypsy identity and expresses the essence of what is eternal in Andalusia.

IT'S OVER WITH EMILIO ALADRÉN

Lorca always hid or denied his homosexuality. Perhaps because of respect for his family, particularly his mother, or because Spanish society had such strict moral codes governing sexual relations. During Franco's reign, many people attempted to explain away Lorca's unjustifiable death, attributing his assassination to the fact that he was a 'queer'. Psychological critics, in their turn, made attempts to explain his works through the lens of homosexuality. In fact, several biographers have pointed out some of his gay relationships, without managing to agree entirely amongst themselves. There is still a lack of consensus between biographers and good friends on this aspect of the poet's life although it is generally agreed that the poet had a relationship with the young sculptor **Emilio Aladrén**.

SAY IT ISN'T SO. THAT YOU'RE NOT GETTING MARRIED

YOU KNOW. LIFE IS FULL OF SURPRISES. I'M IN LOVE AND BESIDES, ELENA'S GOOD FOR ME, SHE'S ABSOLUTELY LOADED. YOU HAVE TO UNDERSTAND, SHE'S AN HEIRESS I FIGHT WITH MY GOOD LOOKS, THE ONLY WEAPON I HAVE. I'M A BEAUTI-FUL MAN AND I DON'T MIND FAVOURS!

Federico, stupefied, turned to leave…

SLAM!

In 1929, acting on the advice of his old professor and friend, **Fernando de los Ríos**, Lorca accompanied him to New York. After brief stays in Paris and London, they arrived on 25 June. The theoretical aim of the trip was for Federico to learn English and familiarise himself with new advances in theatre; in truth, he left to escape the envy of his friends, who tried to discredit the earthiness of his gypsy ballads. Lorca had also been overwhelmed by the success of the *Ballads*, particularly as people had begun to think of him as a gypsy poet. Luis Buñuel, together with Dalí, had poked fun by making a surrealist film, malevolently entitled *Un Chien Andalou* (An Andalusian Dog). Lorca's journey was, therefore, an escape from the bitter side of his own popularity. It was also an attempt to put the emotional turmoil of his failed relationship behind him.

THIS CITY OVERWHELMS, BUT IT DOESN'T STARTLE.

He stayed in New York, confronted by a civilisation entirely different from his own. He wrote poems that would later form the collection *Poet in New York* and began writing two plays: *The Public* and *Once Five Years Pass*. All three were avant-garde works.

'I arrive in this Babylonian city where the immigrants of various races form ghettos. A city that turns its back on nature, where innumerable skyscrapers are like cemetery niches, a city where an unbelievably immense amount of food is consumed, and this immensity is manifested in the vomit and urine of the crowds.'

Lorca's verse changed, as did his images, which became more surreal. He began to use free verse and metaphors that mixed diverse elements which made no logical sense:

Vomit was delicately shaking its drums
among a few little girls of blood
who were begging the moon for protection.

I protect myself with this look
that flows from waves where no dawn
* would go,*
I, poet without arms, lost
in the vomiting multitude.

Lorca at Columbia University

71

A prophet, Lorca foretold the new era of dehumanised technology that was approaching. His new experiences were consolidated in *Poet in New York*, the book he would finish years later. Utterly different from any of his earlier works, within the realms of Spanish surrealism, it was not automatic writing; that is, the poet did not allow his unconscious to flow with no rational control. The sometimes occult images he used spoke of his terrors, of his disagreement with racial segregation, of his loneliness in the multitudes, of his shock at the stock market crash on Wall Street. In 'Dance of Death', he wrote:

*and the bank director looked at
    the pressure gauge
that measures the cruel silence of
    money,
the mask reached Wall Street.*

*The mask will dance between columns
    of blood and numbers,
between hurricanes of gold and the
    groans of laid-off workers
who will howl, dark night, for your
    time without lights.*

The poet prophesied the end of modernity. He also perceived an apocalyptic feeling, stemming from everything that New York encapsulated at the end of one era and the beginning of another.

Lorca had already experienced the universality of Andalusian existence. Now he saw it in the black people in New York, treated with scorn and alienated by American society on the one hand, admired for their music on the other. At this time, the black vaudeville show was taking the place of the white one.

When a black man sings in the theatre, there is a 'black silence', a concave silence...

The black actors always get the best laughs in North America.

When a white actor wants to gain the attention of the audience, he paints himself black, like Al Jolson.

Al Jolson

The black man was a radical theme in *Poet in New York*. Lorca saw black people as an example of oppression, inequality and an imperfect democracy.

AY, HARLEM!

AY, HARLEM!

AY, HARLEM!

No anguish can compare to
* your oppressed reds,*
your blood shuddering amid a
* dark eclipse,*
your violence—garnet, deaf
* and dumb in the half-light,*
your great king imprisoned in
* a janitor's uniform.*

The last poem in the book, 'Song of Negroes in Cuba', tells of black people living in freedom and contentment, much different from the subjugated race Lorca found in New York. In touch with tropical nature, with the flora and fauna, with the sea and the beaches, the black man recovers his origins and regains the power of his race.

> *I, too, wanted to reach Santiago:*
> *the roofs of palm will sing*
> *I'll go to Santiago.*
> *When the palm wants to be a stork,*
> *I'll go to Santiago*
> *and when the banana tree wants to be a jellyfish,*
> *I'll go to Santiago.*

Paper sea and silver coins.
I'll go to Santiago.

When he left the United States on 30 March, the poet had seen and grasped the future of art. As soon as he arrived in Cuba, he spoke his language and found his tongue, and began work on *The Public*. Lorca was attempting to make new theatre. This play proved that during his trip to Paris and his stay in New York, he had indeed familiarised himself with new productions that came from as far off as China. In it he made use of the 'play-within-a-play' device used by Pirandello, and surrealist theatre. After three months in Cuba, Lorca boarded a ship and set sail for Spain.

74

READING IN MADRID:
ONCE FIVE YEARS PASS

In Madrid Federico gave a reading of one of his new plays, *Once Five Years Pass*, to the Chilean ambassador Carlos Morla Lynch, his wife Bebé and his family, who were close friends, plus other selected friends. Their faces registered surprise and disagreement. Federico was convinced that they had not liked it.

MORLA:

BUT IT'S LIKE REALITY AND FICTION ARE ALL JUMBLED UP. THE PLAY SEEMS UNFINISHED I UNDERSTAND THE WORDS THE CHARACTERS SAY, BUT I DON'T KNOW WHAT THEY MEAN.

BEBÉ:

IT HAS A SORT OF SUSPENSE THAT ANNULS THE PASSAGE OF TIME, THAT FORCES THE PAST INTO A PRESENT THAT DOESN'T HAPPEN. IN THAT SENSE IT IS SUCCESSFUL.

GUEST:

BUT THERE SEEMS TO BE NO CONNECTION BETWEEN THE ACTS.

MARTINÉZ NADAL:

The discussion went on and on. It was after three in the morning. Lorca had fallen asleep, with the rolled-up script in his hands.

LA BARRACA AND THE SYSTEM OF 'DOUBLE THEATRE'

After his contact with a select audience who acted as model readers, Federico created a system of 'double theatre': one was unplayable theatre (which the spectator was not mature enough to grasp) and the other was theatre with a realistic story-line, that was meant to be performed (although neither the language nor the techniques conformed to realism). These plays formed the so-called 'rural trilogy': *Blood Wedding* (1933), *Yerma* (1934) and *The House of Bernarda Alba* (1936), finished just months before his death. He also began another book of poems: *The Divan of Tamarit*.

The Barraca caravan, driving through Spain.

In the summer of 1932, the performances of **La Barraca**, the itinerant university theatre group, began after receiving subsidies from the government of the Spanish Republic. Lorca directed, along with his right-hand man, **Rafael Ugarte**. Together they travelled all over Spain, staging adaptations of classical works for the farmers and countryfolk.

These were fruitful and satisfying years. Aside from the fulfilling experience of working with La Barraca, there was also Lorca's relationship with **Rafael Rodríguez Rapún**, an actor and secretary to the nomadic cast who, in spite of his affair with Federico, continued to be a womaniser.

Lorca and the students, together in a small town, were preparing for their performance of *Life is a Dream*, by **Pedro Calderón de la Barca**. The group all wore blue boiler suits with the La Barraca logo. Among them were Federico's sister Isabel and her friend **Laura de los Ríos**, daughter of Don Fernando.

Lorca, dressed as Shadow, recited:

What far off voices, heavens!
from another century sound
mysterious, and still in this one
torment and afflict me so?

Heavens! What far off voices
so mysterious are these,
that in the presence of danger
relieve and console me so?

If from Shadow I went to Dream,
if from Dream to Blame, and from her
to Death who, once present
brought me determined to kill...

79

For Lorca these were both years of maturity in his theatrical profession, and a return to the fun of student life. One of the ways the members of La Barraca entertained themselves was to invent words, to say words that sounded good even if they made no sense—a game created by their director. One night, when the performance was over and the sets taken down, the exhausted group went to the local hotel. Three or four slept in each room. Federico, Méndez de la Calzada and Rapún shared one room. They got into bed and were fast asleep in a matter of minutes. The next morning, at nine o'clock, they woke up in very high spirits.

81

BLOOD WEDDING

Blood Wedding is the first of Lorca's rural tragedies and premièred in Madrid on 8 March 1933. It was a great success. It was the fourth time that one of his plays was staged.

Blood Wedding partially restored the symbolism of *Gypsy Ballads*, with its motifs of life frustrated in death, the knife, the horse, the rider, and the moon as a character. Again, Federico blended the mythical with the everyday. The play, based broadly on newspaper headlines from years earlier, allowed Federico to take up tragedy once more, in this case tragedy that tried to approximate the classic Greek variety. The work was full of poetry, dances and songs which provided the choral element. The characters, with the exception of Leonardo, were nameless archetypes swept along by fate. The apparent realism of the first two acts made the lyricism of the third stand out. The concise language and short sentences pronounced by the characters differed greatly from what had previously been used in Spanish theatre. The first act opens with a conversation between the Bridegroom and his Mother, who recalls the violent deaths of her husband and eldest son.

The Mother gives in to the Bridegroom's request that she accompany him to ask the Bride's father for her hand, and she thinks about the gifts they will bear. The Bridegroom goes off to work in the vineyard.

MOTHER:
DO YOU KNOW THIS GIRL MY SON WANTS TO MARRY?
NEIGHBOUR:
A GOOD GIRL! BUT NO ONE REALLY KNOWS HER. SHE LIVES WITH HER FATHER, SO FAR AWAY, TEN LEAGUES FROM THE NEAREST HOUSE.
MOTHER:
AND HER MOTHER?
NEIGHBOUR:
HER MOTHER I DID KNOW. BEAUTIFUL. HER FACE SHONE LIKE A SAINT'S. BUT I NEVER LIKED HER. SHE DIDN'T LOVE HER HUSBAND.
MOTHER:
WELL! THE THINGS PEOPLE KNOW!
NEIGHBOUR:
PARDON ME. I DIDN'T MEAN TO OFFEND. BUT IT'S TRUE. NOW, WHETHER SHE WAS DECENT OR NOT, THAT I COULDN'T TELL YOU.

85

Once it is discovered that the Bride had been engaged to a boy from the family that killed Mother's husband and son, tragedy is inevitable. This fate is reinforced by folkloric elements and occult symbols which combine to suggest the final tragedy. The newspaper-article tone of the play is thus removed, replaced by an unreal atmosphere in which telluric and celestial forces confront each other, personified by the characters. In the second scene Leonardo's wife and mother-in-law appear, singing a lullaby to the baby in the cra-

dle. The song is an Andalusian one that had obsessed Federico for many years, about a horse who would not drink. He changed the lyrics, however, eliminating the presence of a man and thereby identifying Leonardo with the horse. His passion will not be sated with the love of his Wife. Other warnings can also be seen in the mysteri-ous lullaby.

Lullaby, my baby sweet
dream of the great big horse
who wouldn't drink the water deep.
[...]

Horsie's hooves are red with blood,
Horsie's mane is frozen,
Deep inside his staring eyes
A silver dagger broken.
Down they went to the river bank,
Down to the stream they rode.
There his blood ran strong and fast,
faster than the water could.

When Leonardo arrives, he tells Wife that his horse keeps losing its shoes. It becomes clear from the horse's bulging eyes that, contrary to Leonardo's claims, he has been riding the animal hard and far. Leonardo becomes angry at his mother-in-law's insinuations and at the Shop Girl's enumeration of the many and wondrous things the Bridegroom and his Mother have bought as gifts before going to ask for the Bride's hand. In the next scene, the Mother and her son are at the Bride's house. The realism of the dialogue is obvious. The characters talk of land and what it costs. When the parents meet each other, the Mother of the Bridegroom and Father of the Bride praise their respective children, and in so doing use common rural terms and expressions.

MOTHER:

> MY SON HAS WHAT IT TAKES.

FATHER:

> MY DAUGHTER, TOO.

MOTHER:

> MY SON IS A GOOD MAN. HE HAS NEVER KNOWN A WOMAN. HIS REPUTATION IS CLEANER THAN A SHEET SPREAD OUT IN THE SUN.

FATHER:

AS FOR MY DAUGHTER, WHAT CAN I SAY? SHE MAKES BREAD AT THREE, WHILE THE MORNING SUN IS STILL SHINING. SHE NEVER TALKS SOFT AS WOOL. SHE DOES ALL KINDS OF EMBROIDERY. AND SHE CAN CUT THROUGH ROPE WITH HER TEETH.

MOTHER:

MAY GOD BLESS THEIR HOUSE.

FATHER:

MAY GOD BLESS IT.

When the Bride is alone with the Maid, she lets her indifference towards the Bridegroom be known. The galloping of a horseman is heard, and the conflict established. Leonardo is courting his old girlfriend again, and she is more than interested. The promise of creating new life and carrying on the family line is the fundamental theme of the first act. It will be realised in the grandchildren that the Mother and Father anxiously await.

The second act opens at the Bride's house, which is a cave built into the side of a hill. The Bride is thus tied to the land.

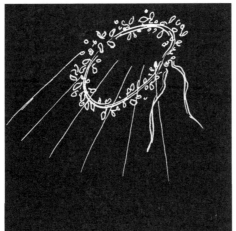

The Bride throws her orange blossom crown to the ground...

MAID: YOU'RE SO LUCKY. YOU'RE GOING TO HOLD A MAN IN YOUR ARMS! YOU'RE GOING TO KISS HIM! YOU'RE GOING TO FEEL HIS WEIGHT!

BRIDE: BE QUIET!

MAID: AND THE BEST PART IS WHEN YOU WAKE UP, AND YOU FEEL HIM BESIDE YOU, AND HIS BREATH CARESSES YOUR SHOULDER, LIKE A NIGHTINGALE'S FEATHER.

BRIDE: WILL YOU BE QUIET?

MAID: BUT CHILD! A WEDDING WHAT IS IT? A WEDDING IS THAT, AND NOTHING MORE! IS IT THE WEDDING CAKE? IS IT THE BOUQUETS OF FLOWERS? NO! IT'S A SHINING BED, AND A MAN, AND A WOMAN!

BRIDE: YOU'RE NOT SUPPOSED TO TALK ABOUT IT!

MAID: THAT'S ANOTHER MATTER. BUT IT'S SO HAPPY!

BRIDE: OR SO BITTER.

This bitterness becomes explicit once Leonardo arrives. He has ridden his horse at top speed to beat all the other wedding guests in order to speak to the Bride in private.

LEONARDO:

TO KEEP QUIET AND BURN IS THE GREATEST PUNISHMENT WE CAN HEAP UPON OUR-SELVES. [...] YOU THINK THAT TIME HEALS AND WALLS CONCEAL, AND IT'S NOT TRUE, NOT TRUE! WHEN THE ROOTS OF THINGS GO DEEP, NO ONE CAN PULL THEM UP!

BRIDE:

I CAN'T HEAR YOU. I CAN'T HEAR YOUR VOICE. [...] IT DRAGS ME ALONG, AND I KNOW THAT I'M DROWNING, BUT I STILL GO ON! [...] AND I KNOW I'M MAD, AND I KNOW THAT MY HEART'S PUTREFIED FROM HOLDING OUT, AND HERE I AM, SOOTHED BY THE SOUND OF HIS VOICE, BY THE SIGHT OF HIS ARMS MOVING.

LEONARDO:

I WON'T BE AT PEACE WITH MYSELF IF I DON'T TELL YOU ALL THIS. I GOT MARRIED. YOU GET MARRIED NOW.

Then the action becomes tighter and faster. The guests arrive and the songs begin, blending poetry and folklore:

Let the bride awaken now
On this her wedding day;
Begin the dance, let flowers now
Your balconies array.

Let the bride awaken now.

Let the bride awaken
To the bright display
Of love's rich green bouquet.
May she awaken now
To trunk and flowering bough
Of laurel on her wedding day!

The Father and Mother speak of grandchildren to come. They are the ones who will till the land, which needs strong arms to tame and punish it. And those arms must belong to the family, to sow the seed. The conversation leads the Mother to dwell on her murdered son.

MOTHER:

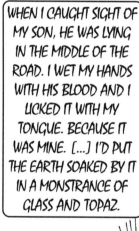

...THAT IS WHY IT'S SO TERRIBLE TO SEE SPILLED BLOOD ON THE GROUND. A FOUNTAIN THAT RUNS FOR A MINUTE, WHEN IT COST US YEARS.

WHEN I CAUGHT SIGHT OF MY SON, HE WAS LYING IN THE MIDDLE OF THE ROAD. I WET MY HANDS WITH HIS BLOOD AND I LICKED IT WITH MY TONGUE. BECAUSE IT WAS MINE. [...] I'D PUT THE EARTH SOAKED BY IT IN A MONSTRANCE OF GLASS AND TOPAZ.

The Bride has retired, to rest for a moment. Suddenly, she cannot be found. Leonardo has passed by silently, hastening her resolve. The end of the act erupts with tension at the revelation that the Bride has run away with Leonardo; the Bridegroom and Mother decide to pursue her, in the name of honour, though they know only blood can cleanse.

The third act, almost entirely in verse, is the most lyrical. The action slows down and the presence of mythical beings—the Moon, the Beggar Woman (death), the Woodcutters and the Fates—floats in the air. They inform the audience of the action taking place, of the hunt for the lovers and of the blood that will spill when they are found. They also elaborate on the lovers' dialogue about their irresistible passion and their fate.

LEONARDO:
...I wanted to forget
And I put a wall of stone
Between your house and mine.

But I'd get on the horse
And the horse would go to your door.
And then the silver wedding-pins
Turned my red blood black,
And our dream began to fill
My flesh with poisonous weeds.
Oh, I'm not the one at fault.
The fault belongs to the earth
And that scent that comes
From your breasts and your hair.

The bloodthirsty Moon brings on the tragedy.

MOON:

The moon places a knife
Abandoned in the sky,
That is a leaden ambush
And longs to be the pain of blood. [...]

And so tonight there'll be
Red blood to fill my cheeks. [...]

Let there be no shadow, no hidden corner
To which they can escape!
For I want to enter a breast
Where I can warm myself!

FIRST GIRL:

BE QUIET, OLD
WOMAN, BE QUIET!

BEGGAR WOMAN:

DEAD,
YES, DEAD.

The symbolic char-
acters confirm the
double death, and
Mother's sense of
catharsis quickly
turns to pain. The
Beggar Woman,
delighted, tells of
the Bridegroom
and Leonardo.

BEGGAR WOMAN:

BOTH OF THEM FELL, AND THE
BRIDE COMES BACK,
HER SKIRT AND HER HAIR
STAINED WITH THEIR BLOOD.

Then the Mother feels all other emotions diminish, even her hatred for the Bride, although she hits her and throws her to the ground. The Bride tries to justify her actions, explaining that she was dragged along by fate:

BRIDE:

I WAS A WOMAN BURNING, FULL OF PAIN INSIDE AND OUT, AND YOUR SON WAS A TINY DROP OF WATER THAT I HOPED WOULD GIVE ME CHILDREN, LAND, HEALTH...

BUT THE OTHER ONE WAS A DARK RIVER, FULL OF BRANCHES, THAT BROUGHT TO ME THE SOUND OF ITS REEDS AND ITS SOFT SONG.

MOTHER:

A WEAK, DELICATE, RESTLESS WOMAN WHO THROWS AWAY A CROWN OF ORANGE-BLOSSOM TO LOOK FOR A PIECE OF BED WARMED BY ANOTHER WOMAN!

BRIDE:

...HONOURABLE, HONOURABLE LIKE A NEWBORN CHILD. LIGHT THE FIRE, YOU FOR YOUR SON, AND I FOR MY...

MOTHER:

WHAT DOES YOUR HONOUR MATTER TO ME? WHAT DOES YOUR DEATH MATTER TO ME?

The play ends with the three women alone together: the Mother, the Bride and the Wife. This tragedy, already seen in other Lorca plays and poems, seems to reflect one of the author's own problems: unconsummated love. The Mother's misfortune is now destined to be repeated in the Wife: husband killed in a fight and only an empty house on the horizon.

LORCA IN BUENOS AIRES

In October 1933, Lorca travelled to Buenos Aires at the urging of the actress **Lola Membrives**, who had achieved great success with *Blood Wedding*. Her invitation was supported by the Society of the Friends of Art, who asked Lorca to give a series of lectures

On arrival, there were his former neighbour Coca and his wife, and Matilde, Pastor's wife, and a group of other people from Fuente Vaqueros.

FEDERICO! FEDERICO

HE'S FROM OUR VILLAGE, HE'S FROM OUR VILLAGE! HE'S FROM FUENTE!

Federico fell in love with Buenos Aires after *Blood Wedding* had a highly-acclaimed second première, which was staged at the enormous Teatro Avenida. The playwright wrote to his parents about it, explaining that the event had been an enormous success.

The great Teatro Avenida is ten times larger than the Teatro Español in Madrid, one of those immense American theatres, and it was occupied by a crowd standing in the aisles and hanging from the ceiling. The theatre has ten boxes, which held the highest of high society, and the rest of the place was packed.

First, I greeted the audience, thanking them for the reception they gave me, and as soon as I stepped onto the stage someone said 'On your feet!' and the whole crowd stood up and gave me a five-minute ovation. Then came the crowning moment. Lola Membrives' performance was absolutely superb, her voice put cracks in the walls and gave everyone goosebumps.

In Buenos Aires, Lorca was reacquainted with old friends such as **Alfredo de la Guardia**, who had been in the audience at the catastrophic opening of *The Butterfly's Evil Spell*; **Gregorio Martínez Sierra**, his first director; and the writer **Victoria Ocampo**, whose publishing house, Sur, published another edition of *Gypsy Ballads* which immediately sold out. He also made friends with several influential poets, critics, writers and painters, including **Pablo Neruda**.

At Amorim's ranch in Montevideo, February 1934

Also there were **Amado Alonso**, who at the time was director of Philology at the University of Buenos Aires, and **Pedro Henríquez Ureña**, who gave out tickets to his disciples at the Higher Institute of Teaching for Lorca's talk on *Poet in New York*. In Montevideo, he met old friends from Granada, such as **José Mora Guarnido** and **Enrique Díez-Canedo**, Spanish Ambassador to Uruguay, and made new friends such as the Uruguayan poet **Juana de Ibarbourou** and the writer **Enrique Amorim**.

Lorca prolonged what was to have been a six-week stay, remaining instead for six months. After *Blood Wedding* had run for several months, all of his known works were then re-staged. On 1 December 1933, a new version of *The Shoemaker's Prodigious Wife* opened, extended with songs and dances. Theatre-goers welcomed the play, so different from *Blood Wedding*, enthused by the poet's fresh versatility. After initial doubts about whether or not to stage *Mariana Pineda*, fearing that the Argentine populace would be uninterested in a topic they were probably unfamiliar with (that of nineteenth-century Spanish political issues), Lorca decided to go ahead with it. To prepare potential audiences, he first broadcast a radio programme and published a brief newspaper column explaining the historical background.

He also prepared a contemporary version of **Lope de Vega**'s play *The Simple-Minded Lady*, starring **Eva Franco** in its 1934 opening, under the title *The Simple-Minded Girl*.

Federico, with Lola Membrives, greeting the public.

Lorca also gave several lectures during his stay. 'Play and Theory of the *Duende*', on 20 October 1933, was the first of these and captivated the audience. *Duende* is an Andalusian inspiration akin to 'soul', and it seems the public in attendance realised that the term was perfectly represented by the poetic voice of the man before them. On 26 October Lorca gave the talk 'How a City Sings from November to November', in which he proved to be an expert on folklore as well as music, and an excellent singer. On 31 October, he spoke on *Poet in New York*, again surprising the audience by showing a surrealist side of himself. Finally, on 8 November, he gave his final lecture, 'Primitive Andalusian Song', about *cante jondo* and its origins. The four talks were all greatly applauded by critics and audience alike.

Soon, Lorca's fame had spread all over Buenos Aires. If he was walking along a street, everyone recognised him. If he was having coffee with a group of friends, all heads would turn to stare.

A dinner at
the Pen Club

PABLO NERUDA:

FEDERICO GARCIA LORCA, A SPANIARD, AND MYSELF, A CHILEAN, ARE NOT THE GUESTS OF HONOUR AT THIS GATHERING OF FRIENDS; RATHER IT IS FOR THAT GREAT SHADOW WHO SANG ABOVE US, AND GREETED, WITH HIS UNUSUAL VOICE, THIS ARGENTINE LAND ON WHICH WE NOW STAND.

FEDERICO:

PABLO NERUDA, A CHILEAN, AND MYSELF, A SPANIARD, HAVE IN COMMON OUR LANGUAGE AND OUR LOVE OF THAT GREAT NICARAGUAN, ARGENTINIAN, CHILEAN AND SPANISH POET RUB N DARIO

...IN WHOSE HONOUR WE RAISE OUR GLASSES IN TOAST.

All of the dinner guests stood for the toast, raising their glasses. Then came thunderous applause.

The lobby of the Teatro Smart. It's midnight. Lorca and **César Tiempo** are leaving the auditorium having just seen a dress rehearsal of César's *I am the Theatre* when they meet the famous tango singer, **Carlos Gardel**:

In Gardel's office:

YOU'LL SEE THE WHOLE THING IS A LIE.
YOU'LL SEE THAT NOTHING IS LOVE.
THAT NOBODY REALLY CARES
STREETWALKER STREETWALKER

CÉSAR TIEMPO:

BOYS! THIS IS UNBE-
LIEVABLE!

Lorca's farewell to Buenos Aires was a sort of all-night party, held in the foyer of the Teatro Avenida, and dedicated to his friends. After several short pieces, he put on a puppet play, *The Little Puppet Show of Don Cristóbal*. In it, he named several friends and critics.

Amado Villar snores like an accordion.
Pablo Neruda snores like a skull
and Rojas Paz snores exactly like Raúl
  González Tuñón.

Don Cristóbal finishes by poking fun at the most important critics of the theatre world:

The critic from the Daily
  snores ever so gaily
and the critic from the Spanish Daily
  snores throughout the function, and
drops his cane with gumption
and makes such a commotion.

On 13 March 1934, Lorca boarded the *Conte Biancamano* for the
return voyage to Spain.

In Madrid Federico put the finishing touches to a new play, *Yerma*, which he then gave to Margarita Xirgu to open at the Teatro Español. At the time there was great political unrest. The fact that Xirgu was a friend of **Manuel Azaña**, the ex-Prime Minister and Republican leader, had serious repercussions. In addition, **Rivas Cherif**, the director, was Azaña's brother-in-law. On 28 December an avant-première was held; it was attended by the writers **Miguel de Unamuno**, **Jacinto Benavente** and **Ramón del Valle-Inclán**. The following day the play opened to a full house and with storm clouds brewing.

In spite of the disturbances, *Yerma* was a huge hit.

Yerma was a tragic poem of sterility. Lorca himself defined it as a tragedy without a plot. It contained long silences, used poetically so that Yerma, and only Yerma, would hear a child crying as she conversed with Victor, a shepherd whom she had been in love with as an adolescent. In fact, he was the only man she had ever loved.

YERMA:

DO YOU HEAR THAT?

VICTOR:

WHAT?

DON'T YOU HEAR CRYING?

NO.

I THOUGHT I HEARD A CHILD CRYING.

YES?

NEARBY. CRYING AS IF HE WERE DROWNING.

I CAN'T HEAR ANYTHING.

IT MUST BE MY IMAGINATION.

The feelings she has for her husband, Juan, are quite different. Her father married her off and she accepted, thinking of the children she would have in the future. Yerma anxiously awaits their arrival and looks with envy and admiration at the young mothers around her. The second act introduces the washerwomen who fulfil the role of the Greek chorus. Their function is to narrate and comment on what has happened and on the lead couple's conduct.

FOURTH WASHERWOMAN:

> THERE'S SOMETHING IN THIS WORLD CALLED 'A LOOK'. MY MOTHER USED TO SAY THAT. A WOMAN DOESN'T LOOK AT ROSES THE SAME WAY SHE LOOKS AT A MAN'S THIGHS. SHE 'LOOKS' AT HIM!

FIRST WASHERWOMAN:

> BUT AT WHO?

FOURTH WASHERWOMAN:

> AT SOMEONE, DO YOU HEAR? THAT'S FOR YOU TO FIND OUT. OR DO I HAVE TO SAY IT LOUDER? AND WHEN SHE'S NOT LOOKING AT HIM, BECAUSE SHE'S ALONE, BECAUSE HE'S NOT RIGHT THERE IN FRONT OF HER, SHE HAS HIS PICTURE IN HER MIND'S EYE.

FIRST WASHERWOMAN:

> THAT'S A LIE!

Yerma drifts further and further away from her husband, despising her empty home. Juan thinks only of gaining more property and of his crops. Yerma goes out to speak to women and to ask about her chances for motherhood. Juan brings two of his sisters to watch over her, but she refuses to speak to them. Later, Victor and his father sell their sheep to Juan.

Yerma agrees to go with Dolores the conjuror to the cemetery, in order to say prayers at night which are designed to leave her pregnant. Juan, who goes with his sisters to search for her, upbraids her and reproaches her for not thinking of her honour.

YERMA: I'M YOUR WIFE, BUT TAKE CARE YOU DON'T PUT ANOTHER MAN'S NAME ON MY BREAST.

JUAN: IT'S NOT ME WHO PUTS IT THERE. YOU PUT IT THERE WITH YOUR BEHAVIOUR, AND THE TOWN IS BEGINNING TO TALK. I DON'T KNOW WHAT A WOMAN IS LOOKING FOR, OUT OF HER HOME AT ALL HOURS.

YERMA: I'M LOOKING FOR YOU! IT'S YOU I LOOK FOR, DAY AND NIGHT, WITHOUT FINDING ANY SHADE WHERE I CAN REST! IT'S YOUR BLOOD AND YOUR HELP I WANT!

YERMA: DON'T PUSH ME AWAY. WANT WITH ME!

JUAN: GET AWAY!

JUAN: STOP IT!

YERMA: SEE HOW ALONE I AM! LIKE THE MOON TRYING TO FIND HERSELF IN THE SKY. LOOK AT ME!

JUAN: LEAVE ME ALONE, I SAID!

The pilgrimage Yerma makes to the Hermitage in an attempt to get God to listen to her is mixed in with the paganism of the Pagan Old Woman who offers to have her son impregnate Yerma. She rejects this offer indignantly. The Saint of the Hermitage is just a pretext used by lascivious men to satisfy their carnal desires with women who want to be made fertile. The dance of the Male and Female is another type of chorus, and serves to personify intercourse between a married woman and a man who will cure her infertility. The tragedy culminates when Juan, drunk, approaches Yerma.

JUAN:

MANY WOMEN WOULD BE HAPPY LIVING THE LIFE YOU DO. LIFE IS SWEETER WITHOUT CHILDREN. I'M HAPPY NOT HAVING THEM. WE ARE NOT TO BLAME.

YERMA:

THEN WHAT WERE YOU LOOKING FOR IN ME?

JUAN:

FOR YOU, YOURSELF.

Juan's words unleash the tragedy. Yerma grabs him by the throat and chokes him to death. Finally she can rest, knowing that she has no hope of ever becoming a mother. Yerma accepts it: she has killed her son.

The following year, Lorca published *Lament for Ignacio Sánchez Mejías* along with *Six Galician Poems*. Xirgu starred in the opening of *Doña Rosita the Spinster or The Language of Flowers* in Barcelona.

Doña Rosita
the Spinster.

In the *Galician Poems*, published after Lorca's return from Argentina, he created a ballad from the story of **Ramón de Sismundi**, a homesick Galician living in anguish in Buenos Aires. There Sismundi suffered as an immigrant, working as a clerk in a shop in Esmeralda Street:

There in Esmeralda Street
sweeping and sweeping away
dust from the cases and boxes.

The ballad alluded to Buenos Aires and the immense plains of Argentina, the lushness of the pampas. The line 'on the banks of the River Plate' is repeated twice. The beginning of the ballad metaphorically unites the Galician musical instrument with the widest river in the world.

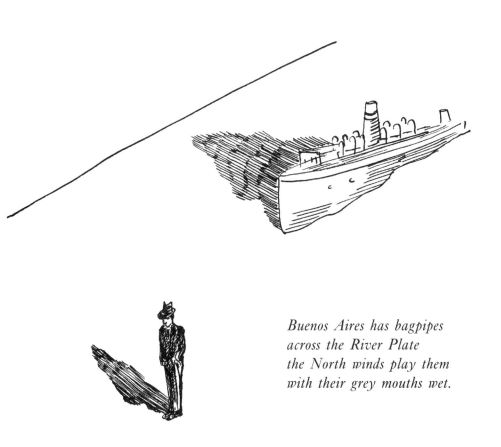

Buenos Aires has bagpipes
across the River Plate
the North winds play them
with their grey mouths wet.

It was not that strange for Lorca to introduce so Spanish and Argentinian a theme into his Galician poems, given that he had only returned a few months earlier from Buenos Aires. Buenos Aires, in addition, was known for having more Galicians than any other city in the world. And, according to the poem, the River Plate poetically closed off access to the road back to Spain with a 'wall of red mud'. Sismundi watches the deceptive shape of his nostalgia disappear—a valley in the lush pampas—and on another mythological plane proves that the city is neither a huge bagpipe nor does it play a 'water muñeira' (muñeira is a Galician dance).

LAMENT FOR IGNACIO SÁNCHEZ MEJÍAS

Ignacio Sánchez Mejías was a famous bullfighter, and a friend of Lorca and of the entire Generation of 27. He was also a writer in his own right, penning articles as well as the plays *Without Reason* and *Skirts*. He lived the life of a gracious and sociable gentleman in Seville, but without ostentation. In fact, he was the man who originally invited the group of poets to Seville in 1927, to celebrate Góngora's anniversary. Ignacio had retired from the ring but returned to it, for a short time, to meet his destiny. On 11 August 1934 he was badly gored in the Manzanares bullring. His death, two days later, was the motivation for Lorca's elegy. The poem was finished on 4 November.

Lorca's favourite picture of Ignacio.

The most original aspect of the *Lament* is its fluctuation between the personal lament for a lost friend and the lament for all the blood ever spilled by bulls and fighters in any bullfight. The mythical sentiment of the man and the bull is centred on Sánchez Mejías, just as every sacrifice is epitomised and relived in every bullfight. Mythical time, which is without history, is therefore seen in the time of the sacrifice: five in the afternoon.

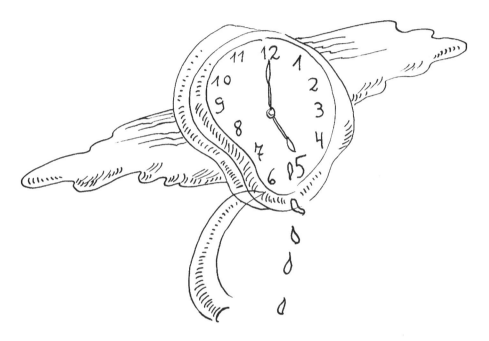

At five in the afternoon.
Exactly five in the afternoon.
A boy fetched a white sheet
at five in the afternoon.

The wind removed the cotton
at five in the afternoon.
The rust sowed glass and nickel
at five in the afternoon.
and a thigh with a forsaken horn
at five in the afternoon.

Silent groups on corners
at five in the afternoon.
The bull alone was glad of heart
at five in the afternoon.

[...]

Ay, terrible five in the afternoon!
It was five by all the clocks!
The shadow of five in the afternoon!

The various occurrences do not follow one another chronologically; they all happen at the same time, a mythical time that brings temporal simultaneity. Lorca explained:

In the middle of the Iberian summer they open the bullrings, that is, the altars. Man sacrifices the brave bull, son of the sweetest cow, goddess of the dawn. Immense celestial cow, continually bleeding mother asks for man's holocaust too, and obtains it. Each year the best bullfighters fall, destroyed, torn by the sharp horns of some bulls who exchange for one terrible moment their role as victims with that of the sacrificers. It seems that by a secret law unknown to man they choose the most heroic bullfighters to take with them.

Tell the moon to come—
I refuse to see the blood
of Ignacio on the sand.

The cow of the old world
passed her sorrowful tongue
over a snout of blood
spilled out upon the sand.

The bulls of Guisando,
almost death, almost stone,
roared like two centuries
weary with treading earth.

NO! I REFUSE TO SEE IT!

He did not close his eyes
seeing the horns come near
but they lifted their heads,
the terrible mothers.

Across the ranches rose
a breath of secret voices
that ranchers of pale mist
called to celestial bulls.

Sánchez Mejías fatally gored in the
Manzanares bullring

According to the poet's brother, Francisco, the night sky was a metaphor within which ranches corresponded to constellations, 'ranchers of pale mist' to the Herdsman constellation, and the celestial bulls to Taurus. The Spaniard felt suddenly impelled by a force which led him in to play with the bull, an automatic reflex he himself could not explain but which was based on the feeling that dead people were watching, leaning against bullring fences made of moonlight.

In the penultimate part of the poem, 'Presence of the Body', the dead man cannot rest. He is carried through 'endless bullrings without walls'. A limitless space where it grows used to death:

> *We are with a laid-out body that is fading,*
> *with a noble form once rich in nightingales*
> *and we see it filled with endless holes.*

The bullring in Seville.

> *Nobody knows you. No. But I sing of you.*
> *I sing of your grace for posterity.*
> *Your profile, your maturity of thought.*
> *Your love for death and the taste of his mouth.*
> *The sadness in your light-hearted courage.*

DONA ROSITA THE SPINSTER
OR THE LANGUAGE OF FLOWERS

Lorca said of the play:

It concerns the tragic course of our social existence: Spanish spinsters.

The piece was set in 1890 and spanned twenty years. Federico said it collected together all the tragedy of Spanish provincial pseudo-refinement, something that would make younger generations laugh but which was profoundly dramatic socially since it reflected what the middle class was like at the time.

Here the concept of comedy left room for drama by accentuating the spinster's marginality in society. When the play's première drew near, Lorca insisted:

On the bills I call it a poem, and that's exactly what it is.

I wanted this comedy to be driven from start to finish by a line of purity.

Did I say comedy? It would be better to say the drama of Spanish pseudo-refinement.

Comedy, drama and poetry all blend into one in *Doña Rosita*, a play that also transcended all of these categories.

In 1924 Lorca was having coffee with his friends Moreno Villa, Dalí and Pepín Bello in the Palace Hotel.

The play's theatricality was rooted in an accumulation of symbols used to communicate the passage of time: songs, clothing styles, and the scenes in which nothing happened. There was the endless provincial monotony. Especially important was the way in which Federico presented time, the invisible character.

In the first act Rosita wears a rose-coloured dress, with bustle, ribbons and leg-of-mutton sleeves. Her hat and parasol complete the outfit. She is beauty at its finest. She clearly corresponds to the rose in the first verse of the poem:

She opens in the morning,
her colour the deepest red.
Afraid of being burned by her,
the dew has quickly fled.

In the second act, the fashion has changed to that of 1900. Rosita wears a bell-shaped skirt. The second quartet explains:

At noon her petals, open wide,
Have all the firmness of coral.
The sun looks down to gaze upon
The splendour of its rival.

In the final act, Rosita
appears wearing a
lighter rose colour, in the
style of 1910...

When birds take to the branches
To announce the approach of sleep,
And evening begins to slip
Into the sea's azure deep.
Then her red grows deadly pale,
Like a cheek by sorrow torn.

Lorca followed the colouring
of the allegorical *Rosa*
Mutabile for Rosita's clothing.

And night, approaching softly,
Blows on a metal horn.
The stars advance across the sky,
The wind no longer calls,
As on the edge of darkness,
Her petals begin to fall.

126

There is not much dramatic action in *Doña Rosita*. In fact it is so minimal as to be fundamentally expressed in the first act alone, when Rosita bids her cousin, to whom she is engaged, farewell. He promises to return for her. The scene is deliberately reminiscent of Zorilla's *Don Juan Tenorio*.

My dream is to see you come, cousin
At night through Granada to me,
When the light's full of salt, cousin,
From longing for the sea.
A lemon grove of yellow,
Jasmine that's white and bloodless,
Stones that kill with their hardness,
All will stop your progress,
And nards spinning like whirlpools
Will fill my house with madness.
Will you ever come back?

YES!
I'LL BE BACK!

In the first act, Rosita is characterised by her impatience. The adverb 'already' and her rapid entrances and exits fit in with the Housekeeper's description of her:

Rosita is not afraid of time. She simply lives it, deceived by the feeling of eternity her youth gives her.

Federico talks to a somewhat older friend who is hopelessly in love with him: **Emilia Llanos**.

AND ROSITA, DOES SHE KNOW? WHAT A SWINE!

NO, FOR YEARS SHE HASN'T KNOWN A THING. HE KEPT WRITING AS IF NOTHING HAD HAPPENED. HE ONLY TOLD THE TRUTH WHEN HIS GODFATHER DIED-HIS AND ROSITA'S UNCLE.

WHAT UNGODLINESS! WHAT INFAMY!

YES. HE LEAVES ROSITA WITH ME HERE IN GRANADA, WITH A ROSARY, A FEW BOUQUETS, THE SOUND OF THE BELLS IN THE ALBAICIN AND A COLLECTION OF FADED, YELLOWING LETTERS FULL OF UTTER AFFECTATION.

IT TAKES FIVE MONTHS TO GET TO TUCUMAN, AND NO ONE RETURNS FROM THERE, SAY THE MAIDS OF GRANADA. AND OUR BOTANY TEACHER USED TO SAY SERIOUSLY: AMERICA IS THE CASTLE YOU GO TO AND NEVER COME BACK FROM.

WHAT ABOUT HER? WHY DIDN'T SHE GO TO HIM?

In the next act, a materialistic century has just begun. Speed is imposed, this time, not by the protagonist but by the outside world. Rosita embroiders her trousseau and waits for letters from her fiancé in America.

Later, the postman arrives with a letter for Rosita. The wedding her fiancé announces in his correspondence is cause for great uproar and fussing amongst the Ayolas and the Spinsters, who are present for Rosita's birthday. It is, however, to be a unique wedding, since the bridegroom will be unable to attend.

The last act is one of disenchantment. While sterility is the central theme in *Yerma*, the death of the son and the seed affect the Bride, the Mother and the Father in *Blood Wedding*. Now, in *Doña Rosita*, it is self-imposed infertility—given that Rosita could have married others and chose not to—that Lorca transmits, enclosing Rosita within her own garden. At the end of the play, she leaves the house and the garden, signifying the definitive abandonment of her place of hope.

I KNEW HE'D GOT MARRIED. BUT I WENT ON RECEIVING HIS LETTERS WITH AN ILLUSION FULL OF SADNESS THAT SURPRISED EVEN ME.

IF NO ONE HAD SAID ANYTHING, IF YOU HADN'T KNOWN, HIS LETTERS AND HIS DECEIT WOULD HAVE FED MY DREAM AS THEY DID IN THE FIRST YEAR OF HIS ABSENCE.

ONE DAY A FRIEND GETS MARRIED, AND THEN ANOTHER, AND YET ANOTHER, AND THE NEXT DAY SHE HAS A SON, AND THE SON GROWS UP AND COMES TO SHOW ME HIS EXAMINATION RESULTS. OR THERE ARE NEW HOUSES AND NEW SONGS. AND THERE I AM, WITH THE SAME TREMBLING EXCITEMENT, CUTTING THE SAME CARNATIONS, LOOKING AT THE SAME CLOUDS. AND THEN ONE DAY I'M OUT WALKING, AND I SUDDENLY REALISE I DON'T KNOW ANYONE. GIRLS AND BOYS LEAVE ME BEHIND BECAUSE I CAN'T KEEP UP, AND ONE OF THEM SAYS:

THERE'S THE OLD MAID ...

...AND ANOTHER ONE, A GOOD LOOKING BOY WITH CURLY HAIR SAYS: NO ONE'S GOING TO FANCY HER AGAIN .

I HEAR IT ALL AND I CAN'T CRY OUT.

Lorca and Xirgu, surrounded by the florists on the Avenue Barcelona:

In the last year of Lorca's life, *First Songs* and *Blood Wedding* were published. But perhaps his most important achievement was to finish **The House of Bernarda Alba**, which, along with *Blood Wedding* and *Yerma* completed the rural trilogy although Federico did not live to see its première.

Madrid. The Count of Yebes' house. His friends acted as 'model readers'

Tears are for when you're alone!
We'll all drown in a sea of mourning.
She, Bernarda Alba's youngest daughter has died a
*   virgin. Did you hear me?*
Silence, silence I said! Silence!

138

MORLA: WHY DID YOU LIKE THAT STORY SO MUCH?

LORCA: BECAUSE THE WOMEN WERE HARMLESS LIKE A RACE OPPRESSED BY MEN. THE WIDOW, ALL MANLY, BOSSED AROUND HER FIVE DAUGHTERS.

MARTÍNEZ NADAL: BUT, HOW DO YOU KNOW THAT?

LORCA: IN BETWEEN HER HOUSE AND MY UNCLE'S HOUSE WAS A DRY WELL. I USED TO GO DOWN THERE AND, BY PUTTING MY EAR TO THE WALL, I'D EAVESDROP ON WHAT WAS HAPPENING ON THE PATIO. THEY'D BE ARGUING AND FALLING OUT WITH EACH OTHER. THE MOTHER YELLED AND SCREAMED. YOU COULD HEAR THE HATRED, THE CONTEMPT. SHE WAS A TYRANT, ALWAYS WORRIED ABOUT WHAT PEOPLE WOULD SAY.

In the meantime, the political climate in Spain grew worse each day.

On 12 July 1936, at 9:30 pm, the anti-fascist lieutenant José Castillo, of the republican Assault Guard, was shot dead. A reprisal was carried out the following day: Castillo's friends kidnapped the right-wing Member of Parliament, Calvo Sotelo, who was found shot in the back of the head a day later. This unleashed the decisive event: **General Francisco Franco** called for a military uprising against the Republic on 17 July. The following morning, in a broadcast from the Canary Islands, he declared martial law.

I ASK FOR THE COLLABORATION OF ALL SPANIARDS.

The Spanish Civil War began.

García Lorca was never affiliated to any political party. This, however, did not keep him from taking a definitive stance, once faced with the military uprising. On more than one occasion, he had declared:

> I am for the party of the poor... but of the good poor.

García Lorca   Raphael Alberti   María Teresa León

He attended political functions, such as the banquet in honour of **Rafael Alberti**, who had recently returned from Russia, and at the function he read a Spanish writers' manifesto against fascism. His sympathy for the Republic was well known but his messages of support would later seal his fate.

On 16 July, the poet left Madrid for Granada, in order to celebrate his and his father's Saint's Day with his family. Rafael Martínez Nadal was with him on that last day in Madrid.

All day, Federico had been unable to decide whether or not to stay on in Madrid. When he finally decided to go to Granada, Nadal accompanied him to the train station and boarded the train to help him get his luggage into the sleeping-car.

* 'Lizard' is said to ward off evil or bad luck.

On 6 August, a squad of right-wing Falangists, supporters of Franco, commanded by **Manuel Rojas**, turned up at the Lorca family country home, Huerta de San Vicente. They searched the house, but, finding nothing of interest, departed. Three days later another squad arrived, this time under the command of a retired sergeant of the Guardia Civil. They were looking for the caretaker whom they found, tied to a cherry tree and whipped. Federico tried to intervene, but they insulted and assaulted him.

PANSY!

LOOK WHO WE HAVE HERE: FERNANDO DE LOS RIOS'S LITTLE FRIEND.

YES. I AM A FRIEND TO ALL OF MY MANY FRIENDS!

The arrival of another squad prevented the violent scene from continuing.

That night, Lorca and his family met at the Huerta de San Vicente with **Luis Rosales**, a young poet who considered Federico his 'maestro'. They discussed where Federico would be safest.

146

What they did not keep in mind was the fact that Luis and his brothers spent all day on the front and came back at nightfall, if and when they could. Federico, therefore, was alone in the company of Luis' sisters and his mother, **Doña Esperanza**, and one of her sisters, **Aunt Luisa**. The women pampered him and made sure he was comfortable, and the poet repaid them in his own inimitable way: he sang songs at the piano and told them exciting stories about his travels. He also spent some time writing and reading books in Luis' library.

At the Huerta de San Vicente, yet another squad had turned up, this time under the command of **Francisco Estévez**. They had orders to detain Federico García Lorca. When Don Federico replied that his son was not at home, Estévez asked abruptly:

> **IF THE SON HAS FLED, WE'LL TAKE THE FATHER IN HIS PLACE!**

> **SIR, MY BROTHER HAS NOT ESCAPED. HIS IS SPENDING A FEW DAYS WITH FRIENDS OF THE FAMILY, THE ROSALES. HE HAS KNOWN THEM FOR YEARS. A FALANGIST FAMILY IF EVER THERE WAS ONE, AS ALL OF GRANADA KNOWS.**

Estévez seemed to calm down and appeared to be a bit put off. He stood to attention, mumbled some excuse and retreated quickly with his troops.

> **COME ON, SHOUT, CLAP!**

In the Rosales' house, Federico played the piano and sang while Aunt Luisa turned down the lights and Doña Esperanza listened.

Detail from a drawing by José Moreno Villa

149

On the afternoon of 16 August, an ex-Member of Parliament from the right-wing Coalition Party, **Ramón Ruiz Alonso**, arrived at the Rosales household, accompanied by two other men. There were no Rosales men present in the house at the time. Doña Esperanza, when she found out that they had come for Lorca, absolutely refused to hand him over. All of the surrounding streets were cordoned off by armed soldiers and assault vehicles.

Miguel Rosales soon arrived and convinced Federico that it was probably in his best interest to go to the Civil Government to clear things up. Surely it was all a mistake. He would accompany the poet to the Palace of Justice to speak to the governor. Federico eventually agreed to leave.

I WON'T BID YOU FAREWELL BECAUSE I DON'T WANT YOU TO THINK WE'LL NEVER SEE EACH OTHER AGAIN.

He left with Miguel Rosales and Ruiz Alonso. **Governor Valdés**, however, was not to be found at the Civil Government building, and Lorca was forced to wait for him to return that night. He was locked into a room on the first floor. Miguel tried to calm him and assured him that he would return with José, his older brother, to get him out of there.

JOSÉ ROSALES:

HOW DARE YOU COME TO MY HOUSE, A FALANGIST HOUSE, TO DETAIN ONE OF MY GUESTS! AND IN MY ABSENCE! I'VE COME TO DEMAND THAT YOU HAND HIM OVER TO ME. I WILL TAKE FULL RESPONSIBILITY.

YOU CAN'T TAKE HIM NOW. HE HAS BEEN ACCUSED BY RUIZ ALONSO OF A SERIES OF CHARGES, AND WE WILL HAVE TO CLEAR UP SOME MATTERS BEFORE RELEASING HIM.

YOU'LL SEE WHAT I DO TO RUIZ ALONSO, THAT DOMESTICATED WORKER, AND HIS DENUNCIATION!

José leaves, slamming the door.

The following morning, José Rosales went to the Military Command, and later to the Civil Government to speak to Valdés.

Governor Valdés had lied to José Rosales when he said that Lorca had been executed on the outskirts of Granada. In the early morning of 18 August, he and an old teacher, **Dióscoro Galindo González**, both handcuffed and taken by guards and Falangists from the Black Squad, were still in the Civil Government building.

The General, surrounded by
military orderlies, had the
phone to his mouth. His voice
was decisive as he gave the
coded reply:

On the ground floor of La Colonia, amidst a large group of prisoners, the poet was overcome. **Javier Tripaldi**, a twenty-two year old who was on guard duty that night, had just informed Lorca that he was to be shot.

The poet looked at him in utter anguish.

Lorca went to a corner of the room and prayed quietly.

The prisoners were ordered to walk ahead. Their handcuffs had been removed.

Suddenly shots were fired and the prisoners fell. The executioner approached for the final blow. Federico tried to sit up and screamed in desperation:

I'M STILL ALIVE!
I'M ALIVE!
ALIVE!
I'M ALIVE!
ALIVE!

The Fountain of Tears

FEDERICO ASSASSINATED BY FALANGIST TROOPS

WITHOUT TRIAL, INNOCENT OF ALL CRIMES, FOR THE SOLE REASON THAT HE WAS A WRITER WHO SUPPORTED THE REPUBLIC AND PRAISED FREEDOM IN HIS WORKS

A final shot hit his body, flipping him over on the ground near an olive grove. Federico's body fell by Fuente Grande, called Ainadamar or 'The Fountain of Tears' by the Arabs, who dis- covered the spring on a road between the vil- lages of Viznar and Alfacar.

THE HOUSE OF BERNARDA ALBA

Years later, *The House of Bernarda Alba* was premièred in Argentina. The play was written for Margarita Xirgu, who had fled in exile to Buenos Aires. Due to the confusion and mayhem brought on by the war, the script took years to actually reach the actress's hands; she received it in January 1945. Two months later, on 8 March, the play opened at the Teatro Avenida, which had been the site of Federico's great successes in 1934 and 1935.

GIRL:

PEPE EL ROMANO WAS WITH THE MEN AT THE FUNERAL

THIRD WOMAN:

A TONGUE LIKE A KNIFE!

BERNARDA:

IT WAS HIS MOTHER WHO WAS THERE. SHE SAW HIS MOTHER. NEITHER SHE NOR I SAW PEPE. BUT WE DID SEE THAT WIDOWER, YOUR AUNT'S FRIEND. WE ALL SAW HIM. IN CHURCH, WOMEN SHOULD LOOK AT NO MAN BUT THE ONE SAYING MASS, AND AT HIM ONLY BECAUSE HE'S WEARING SKIRTS. WHOEVER TURNS HER HEAD IS ON THE PROWL FOR A MAN.

PONCIA:

TWISTED VINE, REACHING FOR THE HEAT OF A MAN!

The play contrasts two parallel plots: the first is seen by the audience; the second is invisible, and it is here that characters who are spoken of, but not seen, act. Such is the case of Pepe el Romano, who is courting Angustias, the eldest of Bernarda's daughters, with a view to inheriting her fortune. Also heard of but unseen are the harvesters, who come from far away to work the land and who pay for the services of Paca la Roseta, the town's only 'bad' woman; and Librada's daughter, who killed her own daughter and hid her beneath rocks where she was discovered by dogs. The visible action revolves around Bernarda, her mother and her daughters, La Poncia, a maid, a few other women and maids, and Prudencia, a woman who pays a visit to the house. The play's conflict arises from the tension between these two contrasting types of dramatic action.

BERNARDA:

A NEEDLE AND THREAD FOR THE WOMEN; A MULE AND WHIP FOR THE MEN. THAT'S HOW IT IS FOR PEOPLE BORN WITH MEANS. WHERE IS ANGUSTIAS?

ADELA:

I SAW HER PEERING THROUGH A CRACK IN THE DOOR. THE MEN HAVE JUST LEFT.

BERNARDA:

ANGUSTIAS! ANGUSTIAS!

ANGUSTIAS:

WHAT DO YOU WANT?

BERNARDA:

IS IT PROPER FOR A WOMAN OF YOUR CLASS TO GO RUNNING AFTER A MAN ON THE DAY OF YOUR FATHER'S FUNERAL MASS?

ANGUSTIAS:

I WASN'T LOOKING AT ANYBODY!

BERNARDA:

WEAKLING! YOU'RE SICKENING!

PONCIA:

BERNADA, CALM DOWN!

Angustias, as the eldest daughter and therefore the inheritor, has tempted Pepe el Romano with her fortune. She is nineteen years older than Adela, who at twenty is the youngest of the sisters. The others are overwhelmed to discover that Bernarda has given Pepe permission to court her daughter, while they will suffer the seemingly endless mourning process imposed by their tyrannical mother. Particularly affected are Adela, who is in love with Pepe, and Martirio, the physically deformed and most complex of the sisters, who oscillates between her desire for Pepe and her inability to come to terms with this desire. Her hatred centres on Adela, over whom she keeps watch.

María Josefa, Bernarda's mother, is another significant character; she might be seen to represent the hidden side of Bernarda. She is kept locked up due to her senile dementia. The sexual repression which underlies Bernarda's power unfolds erotically in María Josefa's insanity. But it is perhaps La Poncia, Bernarda's maid, who best grasps the tragedy which is approaching this group of women.

La Poncia tries to warn Bernarda of what is happening around her. Pepe leaves Angustias's window at half past one, but another window does not close until four in the morning. Obsessive pride will not allow Bernarda to believe what is already apparent to La Poncia. Another dialogue shows how proud she is of her social class. It appears that Martirio could never understand why her suitor had stopped short of courting her. She has convinced herself that she is weak and ugly and carries on with no faith.

PONCIA:

> MARTIRIO IS INCLINED TO FALL IN LOVE, SAY WHAT YOU WILL. WHY DIDN'T YOU LET HER MARRY ENRIQUE HUMANAS? WHY DID YOU SEND WORD TO HIM NOT TO COME ON THE VERY DAY THAT HE WAS GOING TO HER WINDOW?

BERNARDA:

> AND I'D DO IT A THOUSAND TIMES OVER! MY BLOOD WILL NEVER MIX WITH THAT OF THE HUMANAS FAMILY NOT AS LONG AS I LIVE! HIS FATHER WAS A FIELD HAND!

PONCIA:

> THAT'S WHAT COMES OF PUTTING ON AIRS!

In the rural society described by Lorca, men are attracted to women for economic reasons, which dictate marriage. Adela, who has given herself to Pepe el Romano, is willing to live as his mistress after he marries her older sister. But the act brings out the play's tragedy. Martirio interrupts an amorous encounter between Adela and Pepe el Romano in the stable. Adela argues with her sister, who hears a whistle and turns to go back in. But Martirio stands in her way. Bernarda hears their voices and approaches, as the remaining sisters and La Poncia rush over as well. Adela confronts her mother.

ADELA:

THE SHOUTING IN THIS PRISON IS OVER! THIS IS WHAT I DO WITH THE TYRANT'S ROD. DON'T TAKE ANOTHER STEP. NO ONE GIVES ME ORDERS BUT PEPE.

MAGDALENA:

ADELA!

ADELA:

I AM HIS WOMAN.

ANGUSTIAS:

MY GOD!

ADELA:

GET THAT INTO YOUR HEAD AND GO OUT TO THE CORRAL AND TELL HIM. HE WILL BE MASTER OF THIS ENTIRE HOUSE. HE'S OUT THERE, BREATHING LIKE A LION.

BERNARDA:

> THE GUN! WHERE IS THE GUN?

(Runs out, followed by Martirio.)

(A shot is heard).

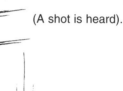

BERNARDA:
(Re-enters)

> I DARE YOU TO FIND HIM NOW.

MARTIRIO:
> THAT'S THE END OF PEPE EL ROMANO.

ADELA:
> PEPE! MY GOD! PEPE!

PONCIA:
> DID YOU KILL HIM?

MARTIRIO:
> NO. HE RAN OFF ON HIS HORSE.

Believing that Pepe el Romano has been killed, Adela hangs herself in despair. Confronted with this tragedy, Bernarda thinks only to impose lies and silence. The traditional Spanish theme of honour, and the fratricide which was on the verge of splitting Spain in two in the Civil War upheld the premise of Lorca's posthumous tragedy. And other significant themes can be found within these. The play's subtitle, 'A Drama of Women in the Villages of Spain' provides the basis for the exploration of other issues. These women with no men, shut away not only in their homes but in mourning, in their class, in their fear of gossip, wither away as time passes them by. The negative view of men and the war of the sexes are two final aspects which complete the panorama Lorca presented.

164

XIRGU:

HE WANTED THIS PLAY TO HAVE ITS PRE-
MIERE IN BUENOS AIRES, AND IT DID; BUT HE
ALSO WANTED TO BE PRESENT AT THE OPEN-
ING, AND FATE WORKED AGAINST HIM.

Margarita Xirgu interrupted the audience, who had started to applaud again; she stood closer to the edge of the stage and continued:

BUENOS AIRES: THE POET'S RESURRECTION

After his tragic death came the long Spanish Civil War and then the silencing of Lorca's voice in his own homeland: his books were banned in all of Spain. Then Losada, an Argentinian publishing house, began in 1938, to publish Lorca's complete works. The texts, which had been in the hands of actors, actresses and friends, formed the first organic body of work which would then be distributed and which created the foundation for Lorca studies. As Spain and Latin America share the same language, the voice of the poet could not be kept quiet.

These days, 'unplayable' theatre is no longer seen as unplayable (scenes from *The Public* are performed in major world theatres). Much of Lorca's poetry was published after his death, from *Poet in New York* to *The Divan at Tamarit*. One collection of poems, *Sonnets of Love*, turned up thanks to the mysterious work of an anonymous publisher.

A never-ending discovery of works continues to surprise us, with numerous children's books, with *Suites*, reconstructed through letters which shed light on the lapse between his first poetry and the *Poem of the Deep Song*, with the unfinished 'Ode and Mockery of Sesostris and Sardanapolus', with the operetta *Lola the Comedienne*, and the exquisite and unfinished *Dreams of my Cousin Aurelia*. In 1997, *Ferias* turned up in Barcelona; it had been a gift from Federico to Mathilde Pomés in 1921.

All of these editions prove that Federico, who seemed like such a bohemian, in fact never stopped working. His poetic and theatrical production surpassed all reasonable limits, given how short his life was, and it continues to bring surprises. His creative activity was also accompanied by a life of elation and intensity. His work was as multi-faceted as his personality, and both were genius.

✳ Bibliography

Works by García Lorca

Barbarous Nights (Legends and Plays), City Lights Books, 1991
The Cricket Sings (Poems and Songs for Children), W.W. Norton & Co, 1980
Deep Song and Other Prose, Marion Boyars Publishers Ltd, 1991
Four Puppet Plays (Edwin Honig ed), The Sheep Meadow Press, 1990
Gypsy Ballads - Hispanic Classics (R.G. Havard ed.), Aris & Phillips Ltd, 1990
How a City Sings from November to November , Cadmus Editions, 1984
Lorca Plays (Blood Wedding/Dona Rosita the Spinster/Yerma), Vintage/Ebury,
    1987
*Lorca Plays (The Shoemaker's Wonderful Wife/The Love of Don Perlimplin/The
    Puppet Play of Don Cristobal/The Butterfly's Evil Spell/When Five Years
    Pass)*, Vintage/Ebury Press, 1990
Lorca Plays (The Public/Play Without a Title/Mariana Pineda), Vintage/Ebury
    Press, 1994
Ode to Walt Whitman & Other Poems, City Light Books, 1988
Once Five Years Pass (& Other Dramatic Works), Station Hill Press, 1995
Poet in New York, Penguin Books Ltd, 1990
The Poetical Works of Lorca, Farrar, Straus & Giroux Books, 1988
A Season in Granada: Uncollected Poetry and Prose, Anvil Press Poetry, 1998
Selected Letters, Marion Boyars Publishers Ltd, 1984
Selected Poems, Penguin Books Ltd, 1997
The Selected Poems of Federico García Lorca, W.W. Norton & Company, 1955
Songs, Duquesne University Press, 1983
Songs and Ballads, Guernica Editions, Inc, 1992
*The Unknown Lorca (Dialogues, Dramatic Projects, Unfinished Plays & a Film
    Script)*, (John London ed), Atlas Press, 1996

Works about García Lorca

Anderson, Reed	*Federico García Lorca*, Macmillan Press Ltd, 1984
Binding, Paul	*Lorca: the Gay Imagination*, GMP, 1985
Crow, John A.	*Federico García Lorca*, University of California, 1945
Edwards, Gwynne	*Lorca*, Marion Boyars Publishers Ltd, 1980
Gibson, Ian	*Federico García Lorca: A Life*, Faber and Faber, 1989
Hernandez, Mario:	*Line of Light and Shadow: the Drawings of Federico García Lorca*, Duke University Press, 1991
Johnston, David	*Federico García Lorca - Outlines*, Absolute Press 1998
Nadal, Rafael Martinez	*Lorca's 'The Public'*, Marion Boyars Publishers Ltd, 1974
Smith, Paul Julian	*The Theatre of García Lorca*, Cambridge University Press, 1998
Stainton, Leslie	*Lorca, a Dream of Life*, Bloomsbury Publishing Plc, 1998

✳ Index

Luis Martínez Cuitiño is Professor of Letters and Principal Researcher at the Council of Scientific and Technical Research (CONICET). He is also in charge of *Letras*, the journal of the Department of Letters of Universidad Católica Argentina.

He has taught in Madrid at the Spanish centres of the University of Southern California and New York University. He spent the years he lived in Madrid researching 20th-century peninsular literature. His own editions of *Gypsy Ballads, Blood Wedding, The House of Bernarda Alba* and *Doña Rosita the Spinster or the Language of Flowers* have been published. He has also written critical works on *Doña Rosita* and *Mariana Pineda*. In addition, he has written numerous articles on the works and biography of García Lorca. He has been invited to speak at many conferences and colloquia on Lorca, both in Argentina and abroad.

Daniela Cancela was born in Argentina and attended the National School of Beaux Arts. In 1967 she received an artist's scholarship from the French government. Since 1969 she has lived in New York, Paris, London and Buenos Aires. As a sculptress, fashion and costume designer and illustrator, her work has been featured in books and in the press (*Vogue, Le Monde, La Nación…*). She has also held many exhibitions including those at the Instituto di Tella, Buenos Aires, The National Museum of Beaux Arts, and The Ginza Art Space in Tokyo.

accept no substitute!

> Great ideas and great thinkers can be thrilling. They can also be intimidating.

That's where **Writers and Readers *For Beginners*®** books come in. **Writers and Readers** brought you the *very first For Beginners*® book over twenty years ago. Since then, amidst a growing number of imitators, we've published some 80 titles (ranging from Architecture to Zen and Einstein to Elvis) in the internationally acclaimed *For Beginners*® series. Every book in the series serves one purpose: to UNintimidate and UNcomplicate the works of the great thinkers. Knowledge is too important to be confined to the experts.

And knowledge, as you will discover in our **Documentary Comic Books,** is fun! Each book is painstakingly researched, humorously written and illustrated in whatever style best suits the subject at hand. That's where **Writers and Readers *For Beginners*®** books began! Remember if it doesn't say…

Writers and Readers®

…it's not an original *For Beginners*® book.

**IRIS MURDOCH
FOR BEGINNERS®**
Bran Nicol
Illustrated by Piero
ISBN 0-86316-401-3
US $11.95
UK £7.99

Iris Murdoch was famous for writing some of the most interesting fiction of the twentieth century: novels that are serious and 'literary', but gripping, funny, and strange, too—a kind of intellectual soap opera. But to call her a novelist tells only part of the story. She was also an eminent philosopher, respected literary critic, sometime playwright, poet, librettist, Dame of the British Empire, Booker Prize winner, Oxford don. Some would even say she was an enchanter, an eccentric, a mystic, a saint, and one of the lovers in 'the love story of our age'...

Iris Murdoch For Beginners® provides an entertaining introduction to this extraordinary writer. It explains the power of novels like *Under the Net, The Bell* and *The Black Prince,* but it also shows that the only way to really understand Murdoch's fiction is through the author and, expecially, the ideas behind it. So this book doesn't just assess Murdoch's achieve-

ment as a novelist and tell the story of her life, career, her sad death and its aftermath. It gives a clear and lively introduction to her philosophy—its context, influences, and main concepts. As a philosopher Murdoch took on many of the most important thinkers (like Plato and Sartre) at their own game, but never departed from her belief that philosophy should be immediately relevant to the kind of experiences each of us go through every day.

So if you've enjoyed Murdoch's novels and want to understand them better, or haven't read them but are thinking about it... If you want to know what existentialism, metaphysics, and moral philosophy are, what 'Eros' and 'ascesis' mean... If you've ever wondered where we should look for moral guidance in a world without God, if you've ever confused obsession with love... **Iris Murdoch For Beginners®** is for you.

new?

**GARCÍA MÁRQUEZ
FOR BEGINNERS®**
Mariana Solanet
Illustrated by
Héctor Luis Bergandi
ISBN 0-86316-289-4

US $11.95
UK £7.99

Nobel Prize-winner Gabriel García Márquez is Latin America's most powerful literary symbol. In three decades, his novel *One Hundred Years of Solitude* has sold over twenty million copies in more than thirty languages, to become the most famous and widely-read novel in Spanish since Cervantes' *Don Quixote*.

García Márquez For Beginners® introduces readers to the man and his 'magical realism', a style that expresses Latin American life and culture in many different layers of human perception.

Gabriel García Márquez has pledged that everything he writes comes out of the real world, including gypsies on flying carpets, a woman ascending to heaven, body and soul, and a priest who levitates when he drinks chocolate.

Throughout his career, from 'The Story of a Shipwrecked Sailor', which first brought national acclaim as a journalist, through the many novels, short stories, writings for cinema to the winning of the Nobel Prize for Literature in 1982 as well as his political/human rights activities, García Márquez has remained an intensely private individual.

This book pays an essential and illuminating visit to the life and works of the Colombian writer who has been described as 'the world's most important living writer' and who is said to represent 'the voice and the spirit of Latin America'.

what's

**GARCÍA LORCA
FOR BEGINNERS®**
Luís Martínez Cuitiño
Illustrated by
Delia Cancela
ISBN 0-86316-290-8

US $11.95
UK £7.99

1998 marked the centenary of the birth of one of Spain's brightest stars in the fields of poetry and drama, Federico García Lorca. His poetry never goes out of print and his plays still have an impact on audiences throughout the world. Lorca or 'Federico', as he was known, was born in Granada in 1889 and was executed, without trial, at the age of thirty-eight by the Falange at the start of the Spanish Civil War.

Lorca was one of the most influential and talented members of the avant-garde movement of his generation. His chilling and compelling drama *Blood Wedding* established him as the dramatist who revived Spanish-speaking theatre.

Lorca appealed to all levels of Spanish society; he merged popular art forms such as gypsy songs and lyrics with classical poetry and music.

In **García Lorca for Beginners®**, Luis Martínez Cuitiño analyses Lorca's work within the context of his life—a life filled with passion and drama—while Delia Cancela's illustrations compliment the text by recreating the line and style of Federico's own drawings.

**RUDOLF STEINER
AND ANTHROPOSOPHY
FOR BEGINNERS®**
Lía Tummer
Illustrated by Lato
ISBN 0-86316-286-X

US $11.95
UK £7.99

At the dawn of the twentieth century Rudolf Steiner created Anthroposophy, the 'spiritual science' that opposes the blindly science-believing, materialistic ideology inherited from the previous century. In so doing, he introduced a truly humanistic concept. Based on a profound knowledge of the human being and his relationship with nature and the universe, Anthroposophy has not only been able to provide renewing impulses to the most diverse spheres of human activity, like medicine, education, agriculture, art, religion, etc., but is also capable of providing answers to the eternal questions posed by mankind, towards which the 'natural sciences' remain indifferent: what is life? where do we come from when we are born? where do we go when we die? what sense has pain and illness? why does some people's destiny seem unjust?

Rudolf Steiner and Anthroposophy for Beginners® describes this universal genius' solitary growth from a childhood in the untamed beauty of the Austrian Alps to the sublimities of human wisdom.

new?

EASTERN PHILOSOPHY
FOR BEGINNERS®
Jim Powell
Illustrated by Joe Lee
ISBN 0-86316-282-7

US $11.95
UK £7.99

Eastern philosophy is not only an intellectual pursuit, but one that involves one's entire being. Much of it is so deeply entwined with the non-intellectual art of meditation, that the two are impossible to separate.

In this accessible survey of the major philosophies of India, China, Tibet and Japan, Jim Powell draws upon his knowledge of Sanskrit and Chinese, as well as decades of meditation. Whether tackling Buddha, Confucius, Lao Tzu, Dogen, the Dali Lama or Patanjal— Powell's insights are deeply illuminating.

All the major philosophies of India, China, Tibet and Japan are explained and the spiritual rewards and intellectual challenges of Eastern philosophy are revealed in this visually stunning book.

This is an exceptionally beautiful **For Beginners®** book, with 19th-century engravings throughout.

Everyone—from beginner to expert—will find **Eastern Philosophy for Beginners®** a beautiful and insightful overview.

PIAGET
FOR BEGINNERS®
Adriana Serulnikov
Illustrated by
Rodrigo Suarez
ISBN 0-86316-288-6

US $11.95
UK £7.99

Jean Piaget's theory of intellectual development is a result of his life's work, spanning almost 80 years of study. His contribution to the field of child psychology is equal to that of Sigmund Freud's achievements in psychiatry. Piaget's aim was to find the answer to the epistemological question: how do you construct human knowledge? Or: how do you acquire precision and objectivity?

Through interviews and tests with children (including his own), Piaget and his colleagues studied the acquisition and development of knowledge in the course of childhood and adolescence, from which he developed his theory of genetic psychology. His work has inspired numerous studies in the fields of education and developmental psychology.

Piaget for Beginners® investigates the key moments of the scientist's life, which are also landmarks in his own personal and professional development.

How to get original thinkers to come to your home...

Individual Orders

US
Writers and Readers Publishing, Inc.
P.O. Box 461, Village Station
New York, NY 10013
www.writersandreaders.com

UK
Writers and Readers Ltd
PO Box 29522
London N1 8FB
Phone: 020 7226 2522
Fax: 020 7359 1406
begin@writersandreaders.com
www.writersandreaders.com

Trade Orders

US
Publishers Group West
1700 Fourth St.
Berkeley, CA 94710
Phone: 800.788.3123
Fax: 510.528.9555

Canada
Publishers Group West
250 A Carlton St.
Toronto, Ontario M5A2LI
Phone: 800.747.8147

UK
Littlehampton Book Services Ltd
Faraday Close
Durrington
Worthing, West Sussex BN13 3RB
Phone: 01903 828800
Fax: 01903 828802
orders@lbsltd.co.uk

South Africa
Real Books
5 Mortlake St.
Brixton, 2092
Phone: 2711 837 0643
Fax: 2711 837 0645

Australia
Tower Books
Unit 9/19 Rodborough Rd.
French Forest NSW 2086
Phone: 02 9975 5566
Fax: 02 9975 5599

SHIP TO (NAME)

ADDRESS

CITY   STATE   ZIP

COUNTRY

TELEPHONE (DAY)   (EVENING)

To request a free catalog, check here: ☐

Title	Quantity	Amount

SUBTOTAL

New York City residents add 8.25% sales tax

Shipping & Handling: Add $3.50 for 1st book, $.60 for each additional book

TOTAL PAYMENT